ADVICE ON TRIAL

ALSO BY JOY STEPHENSON-LAWS

Your Labs Are Fine. You're Not.

Secrets That Sparkle (and Secrets That Sting)

From Chains to Wings: A Poetry Revolution for Healing

Minerals: The Forgotten Nutrient

IN THE COURT OF CLARITY

ADVICE ON TRIAL

The Beliefs You Inherited but Never Examined

With the Feel. Pause. Act.™ framework

JOY STEPHENSON-LAWS, JD

Published by Proactive Health Labs

ISBN (hardback): 979-8-9939740-8-8

ISBN (paperback): 979-8-9968202-0-7

ISBN (ebook): 979-8-9939740-9-5

First edition, 2026

Cover and interior design by Milan Fritzinger.

Printed in the United States of America.

To learn more about the author, visit Proactive Health Labs: phlabs.org/coaches-counselors/joy-stephenson-laws

For my mother, Gladys.

She gave me many of the sayings in this book, and what she knew kept me alive. That I can now ask whether they still serve me is her gift too.

CASE NO. 606692

THE DOCKET

The Cases Before You

INSTRUCTIONS TO THE JURY

This book asks you to sit in a courtroom that belongs to you.

You will not be weighing strangers' lives or distant evidence. You will be considering sayings that have been part of how you think and live. Some came from people you trusted, others from stretches when you were only trying to survive. A few arrived so early that they feel less like ideas you could question than like parts of your personality.

In any other courtroom you would never be seated on this jury. You know the witnesses personally. You were raised by several of them. A juror this close to the case would be struck before lunch. Here, that closeness is the qualification. You will hold every seat in this room, jury and judge both. No one else can hear this testimony from inside your life, and no one else's verdict would stand. You are not asked to be impartial. You are asked to be honest, which is harder.

The task is simple to describe and difficult to do. As you read, notice which sayings you repeat out loud and which ones you carry quietly, and pay attention to any you obey even when something in you resists. Then ask whether they are still true enough for the person you have become.

You can move through the book in any order that helps you be honest. You might begin with the first count and read straight through. You might open instead to the saying that has been pressing hardest on your life lately and begin there. You do not need a fixed sequence to do this work, but you do need a willingness to stay with what you see.

At the end of each count you will find three questions, and after them a page marked Jury Room. Stop there long enough to write something down, or at least to think the questions through before you turn past them. Those pauses are where the verdict starts to form. If you pass them by, the book may still be interesting, or even moving, while the old sayings go on making your decisions for you and you call the experience reading.

At some point a chapter is likely to unsettle you. A familiar piece of advice will be examined from an angle you have never used, or one of your loyalties will be named in a way that does not feel comfortable. If that happens, do not treat the feeling as a mistake. You are allowed to close the book for an afternoon and come back when you can see more clearly. A verdict reached after a pause is more reliable than one reached in the middle of a reaction.

Throughout, remember this: the aim is not agreement with the author. The aim is clarity in your own life. If a conclusion offered here does not fit your experience, note the gap and consider why. You are allowed to keep a saying that this book questions. You are also allowed to retire a saying that has been praised your whole life.

By the end, some of these beliefs will still be standing. A few may turn out not to belong in your house at all. What matters is that you will have seen them clearly before letting them stay or asking them to go. In courtroom terms, your work here is simple to name and difficult to do: feel what the testimony stirs in you, pause long enough to cross-examine it, and act only on the verdicts that the evidence can bear.

Most of the rulings you live by now were entered years ago by default, the way a court rules when no one shows up to contest the claim. This time, you are here.

Court is now in session.

OPENING STATEMENT

The Things We Never Put on the Stand

Somewhere along the way, somebody told you how life works. Maybe it was your mother at the stove, saying family is everything. Maybe it was a teacher who told you to follow your heart, or a coach who said what doesn't kill you makes you stronger, or a quote you saw on a screen at eleven at night that landed so squarely you sent it to three people before you'd finished reading it. You didn't sit down and decide to believe these things. They arrived. They felt true. And because they felt true, you filed them away as true and built parts of your life on top of them.

This book is about going back to look.

Here is the question underneath every page: what am I carrying that I've never stopped to examine? Not the big convictions you could defend in your sleep. The quiet ones. The advice so familiar it stopped sounding like a claim and started sounding like the weather.

I spent more than forty years as a lawyer, and the one habit that work burns into you is this: the statement everyone accepts without blinking is exactly the statement worth questioning. In a courtroom you don't get to wave a thing through because it sounds right. You put it on the stand. You ask where it came from. You ask what it leaves out. You ask whether it holds up when the pressure is on, or only when the room already agrees. Then, and only then, you decide what to do with it.

Most of the advice we live by has never once been cross-examined. That is not the same as saying it's false, and this is the part people get wrong, so I want to be plain about it. I am not here to tell you the sayings you grew up with are foolish, or that the people who handed them to you meant you any harm. Most inherited advice isn't wrong. It's incomplete. It's true on a Tuesday and dangerous on a Friday. It's the right counsel for one season of a life and the exact wrong counsel for the next. The trouble was never the advice. The trouble is that we swallowed it whole, once, a long time ago, and never chewed.

• • •

So this book teaches a way of chewing. There are three moves, and together they make up the framework I call Feel. Pause. Act.™

In courtroom terms, the feeling is the first witness. The pause is the cross-examination. The act is the ruling made visible.

FEEL. PAUSE. ACT.

FEEL comes first, and it comes first on purpose. When a piece of advice lands on you, or grates against you, that reaction is not noise to push down and it is not a feeling to apologize for. It is information. It is the first evidence you get. If a saying everyone loves makes something in you tighten, that tightening is telling you where to dig. You don't have to obey the feeling, and you don't have to silence it. You have to read it.

PAUSE is the cross-examination. Here you take the comfortable saying and ask the lawyer's questions. Is it true? Is it always true? Who taught me this, and what did it cost them? What is it quietly leaving out? Does it still serve the person I am now, or only the person I was when I first believed it?

ACT is the part most books like this one forget. Examining a belief and feeling clever about it changes nothing. The point is to do something on the other side of the thinking. Keep what holds up. Revise what doesn't. Then live differently, in some small and concrete way, because of what you found. A belief you have examined but never acted on is just a belief you have examined.

The book moves through six kinds of inherited wisdom: the beliefs that taught you love and loyalty, the armor that helped you survive, the inner voices you were told to trust, the stories people hand you about pain, the sayings that push you toward ambition and action, and finally the large claims about truth, freedom, happiness, perspective, and what it means to be right.

Each count ends with a pause for deliberation, and a page to write on. Not to force a conclusion, but to let you hear what the testimony stirred before you move on.

You'll notice I am not going to do all of this for you.

For each piece of advice in this book I'll tell you why it grips us, I'll put it on the stand, and I'll offer a fuller and messier and more honest version. But the verdict is yours. I don't live in your house, your marriage, your body, or your history. Some chapters will feel like they arrive at an answer. Others will leave you inside the question.

By the time you reach the last page, you won't only have read about Feel. Pause. Act. You will have done it twenty-four times, on the exact sayings that have been running quietly in the background of your life. That is the whole design. Not a framework you admire. A habit you keep.

Let's call the first witness.

IN THE COURT OF CLARITY

COUNT ONE

THE PEOPLE,
Plaintiff,
v.
THE BELIEFS THAT TAUGHT YOU LOVE AND LOYALTY,
Defendant.

CASE NO. 606692

JUDGE: YOU

The charge: **that they taught you to mistake obligation for love.**

Love and Loyalty

WITNESSES IN THIS COUNT

The beliefs in this count are the oldest ones you carry, the ones that arrived before you were old enough to question anything. Nobody sat you down and made the case for them. They came in through the people who loved you, or said they did, and by the time you could think for yourself they were already part of how you saw the world.

They are all, in one way or another, about loyalty.

Who you owe, and how much.

Loyalty is rarely presented as a question. It is presented as proof. Proof that you are grateful. Proof that you are good. Proof that you remember where you came from and who stood there first. So when an old bond asks something of you, it does not always sound like a request. Sometimes it sounds like love itself, sometimes like the price of belonging.

The sayings in this count pull on that loyalty from different directions. Family is everything asks you to honor the people who came first. Good people put others first asks you to prove your goodness by making yourself available. When your past calls, don't answer asks you to cut a tie, to refuse the pull of where you came from and who you used to be.

Set them side by side and you can see the real question underneath them. It is not whether loyalty matters. Of course it does. A life with no loyalty in it would be thin and cold. The question is which loyalties still deserve you, and which ones you have been keeping out of guilt, habit, fear, or the old belief that leaving something behind means you never loved it properly.

Loyalty runs in more directions than we usually admit. Outward, to family and to the people who need us. Backward, to our origins and to the person we used to be. Inward, too, though that is the loyalty we are often taught to mistrust first.

A pull backward can feel exactly like love, which is what makes it hard to examine. Refusing to answer the past can look like betrayal when it is closer to survival. Answering it can look like loyalty even when it quietly costs you everything you have built since.

None of these sayings is wrong. Each one protects something real. But each one, left alone, will decide your life for you and call that devotion.

So carry one question through this count:

THE QUESTION BEFORE YOU

When loyalty asks something of you, is it asking because the bond is worth keeping, or only because the bond is old?

THE FIRST WITNESS

"Family is everything."

DIRECT EXAMINATION

This is not a saying you hear so much as one you absorb. It arrives before language does, in who held you when you cried and whose face you looked for across a crowded room. By the time anyone says the words out loud, you already believe them in your body.

And the words promise something the rest of the day rarely does. Out there you are useful or you are not, and you can be replaced. "Family is everything" says there is one place where none of that applies, where you belong by birth rather than by merit, where the love arrived before you did anything to earn it. At the end of a hard week, that sentence is a lit kitchen window. Of course we love it. We need it to be true.

Often it is. Family can be the people who know the least flattering version of you and stay in the room anyway. That is not a small thing. For a great many people, it is the closest they ever come to safety.

And if that was not your family? The sentence pulls anyway, sometimes harder. For the reader whose house was loud in the wrong ways, or empty, "family is everything" names a hunger more than a memory, the ache of looking at someone else's lit window from the street. That ache doesn't make the saying naive. It shows how deep the need runs.

So if something in you softened reading this, notice it. And if instead it pressed on a bruise, the old wish for the family you didn't get, notice that too. Either way, what surfaced is real, and it is the first witness. Hold onto it, because we are about to test the sentence, and what you felt is part of what the sentence has to answer for.

CROSS-EXAMINATION

Look at the word "everything." That is the word doing the work, and the damage.

If family is everything, then nothing stands outside it to measure it against, and no standard exists that it can fail to meet. Anything that cannot fail cannot be questioned. That is the moment the sentence quietly stops being a comfort and becomes a leash.

The same words that reassure a loved child are the words that keep a grown person tethered to someone who is hurting them, because "but they're family" has closed more honest conversations than almost any phrase we own. It tends to get handed to you at the exact moment you are trying to set a limit, and it is built to make the limit feel like betrayal.

I know this pull firsthand. The companion to "but they're family" is "blood is thicker than water," and for years that proverb kept me feeling guilty whenever I put distance between myself and relatives who had given me every reason to. One of them used my Social Security number to open a credit card I never authorized. At another's Christmas dinner I showed up and sat through the meal feeling unmistakably unwelcome. The saying did not care what they had done.

It asked only whether they were blood, and because they were, it told me the fault was mine for pulling away.

So no, the sentence isn't false. It is incomplete. It forgets to say which family, and on what terms.

A fuller, messier truth

Here is the version that survives cross-examination, and it is deliberately not as tidy as the original:

Family is one of the most powerful forces in a life, strong enough to hold you up and strong enough to do lasting harm, which is the exact reason it cannot be everything.

Blood can explain the bond, though plenty of real families are chosen rather than born. History deepens it, and love can make it sacred. But none of those things removes the need for terms. Family does not stop being family because you name what you can and cannot carry. Sometimes terms are the only way love survives without turning into injury.

That does not fit on a coffee mug, and that is the point. The original was clean because it was incomplete. The truth has edges.

FEEL. PAUSE. ACT.

FEEL. Go back to whatever showed up when you read the sentence, the softening or the flinch. If it warmed you, ask what exactly you are grateful for, because that is the thing worth protecting. If something tightened, that tightening knows something you have not yet said out loud. Don't argue it away. Read it.

PAUSE. Run the one question the sentence is built to stop you from asking: What is being asked of me, in the name of family, right now? And would I ask the same of someone I love?

ACT. Choose one family relationship and say its actual terms out loud, even if only to yourself in the car. "I will keep showing up for Sunday dinner. I will stop lending money that never comes back." Or say the harder kind, about how you let yourself be treated: "I will visit. I will not explain my life to people who treat my choices as family property."

§

Terms are not betrayal. Terms are what let love survive contact with reality. A relationship with no terms isn't unconditional. It is only undefended.

THE SECOND WITNESS

"Good people put others first."

DIRECT EXAMINATION

For a lot of us this wasn't taught so much as rewarded. You were the helpful one, the child who never added to the pile. You got loved for it, or at least praised, and somewhere those two things blurred. By adulthood you don't experience "put others first" as a rule you follow. You experience it as who you are. It is wired into your sense of being a good person at all.

And it holds communities together. Someone has to bring the casserole, sit with the dying, cover the shift, remember the birthday. A world where nobody put anyone else first would be unbearable, and you know it, because you have been on the receiving end of someone's generosity on a day you couldn't stand up on your own. The instinct is real and it is good.

So notice what came up when you read the line. If it was a warm flush of recognition, that is worth knowing. But if what came up instead was a wave of tiredness, pay closer attention to that one. The tiredness is not a character flaw. It is information your principles have been refusing to let you read.

The trouble is one small word: first.

Not “others matter,” which is plainly true, but others first, by reflex, every time. Run that forward a few decades. If you are always the first to give and always the last to be given to, you have not built a life of generosity. You have built a hierarchy with yourself at the bottom, and you are the one who keeps building it, every time you wave off your own needs as less urgent than everyone else’s.

Here is the distinction the saying quietly erases. Generosity and self-erasure look identical from the outside and feel nothing alike from the inside. Generosity is chosen, and it comes from having enough to share. Self-erasure is compulsive, and it comes from a fear that you are only lovable while you are useful. One fills you even as you give. The other empties you and calls the emptiness virtue. The saying praises both as the same act, and they are not.

And there is a cost it never mentions. The person who always goes last trains everyone around them to expect it. The giving stops being seen, the resentment goes underground, and one day either the well runs dry or the giver curdles into a martyr keeping a score no one else knew was being kept. A self worn down to nothing does not have more to give. It has less.

I have never been the one who gives herself away like this, but I have watched it up close, in friends I love. They will track everyone else’s health and let their own go untended, making sure everyone around them sees a doctor while their own symptoms sit and wait. The people around them call it devotion. And I have watched that devotion hollow them out, until the one who kept everyone else well had no one looking after her, and had long since stopped looking after herself.

Caring for others is a real virtue, maybe the central one, and none of this is an argument against it. The saying just stops one name short of the list, and the name it leaves off is yours.

A fuller, messier truth

Good people care for others and count themselves among the people who deserve care. Generosity is not measured by how much of yourself disappears in the giving. It is measured by whether the giving is chosen, honest, and sustainable. The virtue lives in the narrow middle, where you give from enough instead of from empty, and where your own need is not treated as an embarrassing interruption in everyone else's life. The aim was never to put yourself first every time. It was to stop pretending you are not in the room.

FEEL. PAUSE. ACT.

FEEL. Go back to whichever it was, the glow or the fatigue. If it was fatigue, sit with it for a second instead of explaining it away. Your body has been keeping a ledger your conscience won't let you open. Let it show you one line.

PAUSE. Ask the question the saying is built to keep you from asking. Am I giving from fullness or from fear? And if I am always last in line, who is caring for the person who cares for everyone?

ACT. Pick one request this week that you would normally absorb without thinking, and decline it with no essay of justification attached. Just "I can't take that on this week." Or do the harder version: name one of your own needs out loud to someone who could actually meet it, and then let them. "I need you to take this one." Or, if availability has become your proof of goodness, say it out loud too: "I will help when I can. I will not prove my goodness by being available every time someone asks." The behavior is small on purpose. You are practicing being one of the others, once, deliberately.

§

Where your own line sits between generosity and self-erasure is not mine to draw. I don't know your people, your obligations, or what you can carry, and a line drawn from outside your life would be worthless. Giving from love and giving from fear do feel different in the body, and you have felt both. That difference is your first evidence, though not quite a verdict: fear is good at dressing up as duty, and a tired yes can feel almost like a generous one. Read it honestly, and act from what you find.

THE THIRD WITNESS

"When your past calls, don't answer. It has nothing new to say."

DIRECT EXAMINATION

This one feels like freedom. It hands you permission to stop being dragged backward, to quit picking at the old wound, to stop replaying the argument you lost or the person who left. If you have ever lain awake running the same scene for the hundredth time, you know exactly the loop it promises to cut. Don't answer. Let it ring. You don't owe the past a conversation.

And sometimes that is precisely right. There are people from your past you should not pick up for, and there are memories that offer nothing but a fresh coat of pain. The instinct to guard your present against all of that is a good one, and the relief you feel reading the line is real.

So notice that relief. But notice too if something underneath it flickers, a small unease, the sense that you are being told to slam a door you are not sure should be shut. That flicker is also information.

The line makes one quiet assumption: that the past only ever calls to drag you back. That it is always a trap and never a teacher.

But the past has two reasons for calling, and the saying only knows one of them. Sometimes it calls to pull you under, and yes, let that one go. And sometimes it keeps calling for the opposite reason. It calls because there is something in it you never actually picked up, a lesson you have not learned, and it will keep coming back, in the same fight with a different face and the same heartbreak in a different bed, until you finally answer once. Refusing that call is not freedom. It is avoidance wearing the costume of a boundary, and the thing you will not look at does not leave. It moves into the basement and starts running the house.

Here is the difference the saying cannot make for you. There is the past person, the ex whose number you are right not to dial, the one who only calls to reopen the same wound. And there is your own past, which is not a person at all but a pattern or an old grief: the habit of reaching for people who can't quite love you back, the loss you keep walking the long way around. That past is not asking to move back in. It is asking to be understood so it can finally leave you alone.

My own version of this call is a gentler one, and it still tests me. A friend I have known since I was sixteen wanted more than friendship back then, and every so often, long after I married a man I love, he checks in to ask, in so many words, whether the door is really closed. There is a real pull in it: being wanted by someone who knew you that young flatters a part of you that never grows up, and it whispers about the road you didn't take. But a pull is not a verdict. I let that call ring, not because he is unkind, but because what it offers is a past I already chose to leave.

Some calls really should go unanswered, and the advice earns its keep there. Where it fails is at the switchboard: it cannot tell the call that pulls you under from the call that keeps ringing because it still has something to teach you.

A fuller, messier truth

The past isn't always trying to drag you back. Sometimes it is just trying to be understood. So when it calls, find out which call it is. If it is only there to hurt you again, let it ring. But if it keeps returning in the same recurring fight and the same familiar ache, answer it once, long enough to learn what it came to say, and then come back to the present. The skill is the difference between a phone call and a forwarding address. You are allowed to listen. You are not required to move in.

FEEL. PAUSE. ACT.

FEEL. Go back to the relief, or to the flicker of unease beneath it. If there was unease, the door you are being told to shut may have something behind it you have not dealt with, and the unease may be the part of you willing to admit it.

PAUSE. Ask the question the saying skips. Is this the past trying to drag me back, or trying to teach me something I keep refusing to learn? Is this a person I should not re-engage, or a pattern I have never understood?

ACT. If it is truly a person who only harms you, choose the clean boundary and make it plain. "I will not reopen this conversation." But if it is your own pattern calling, answer it once, on purpose. You can study a pattern without picking up the phone. Write the lesson down in a single sentence: "What this keeps trying to teach me is ___." For one person that sentence reads, "I confuse being chosen with being loved." Then close the notebook and do one small thing in the present. Make the tea, or call someone who lives in your today. You answered. Now you come back.

§

Only you can say which call this is. I'll just warn you that the past is the worst place to trust a feeling at face value, because the body keeps mistaking the familiar for the safe. The person who is bad for you can feel like home precisely because you have been there before. So when it rings, don't only ask how it feels. Ask what it is. Then decide whether to pick up.

JURY DELIBERATION · COUNT ONE

What Did Love Teach Me to Carry?

You have heard three sayings about who you owe, and how much. Before you move on, sit for a moment with what they stirred.

Which loyalty have you never questioned because questioning it felt like betrayal?

Where are you still paying a debt that was settled long ago, or was never yours to begin with?

What would it cost to be loyal to yourself here, and who first taught you to call that selfishness?

Some of these bonds you will keep, gladly. Others you may have outgrown before you noticed.

THE RULING

*The ruling is **yours.***

JURY ROOM

Use the space below to respond to the deliberation questions, record what surfaced, or put your ruling into words.

IN THE COURT OF CLARITY

COUNT TWO

THE PEOPLE,)
) CASE NO. 606692
Plaintiff,)
) JUDGE: YOU
v.)
)
THE ARMOR THAT HELPED YOU SURVIVE,)
)
Defendant.)

The charge: **that they kept the armor on long after the threat was gone.**

Survival and Armor

WITNESSES IN THIS COUNT

Not all advice arrives as wisdom. Some of it arrives as armor. It does not try to make you good or wise or happy. It tries to keep you from being hurt in rooms that were never built with your safety in mind.

Some of this armor was handed to you by people who had already been cut in those rooms and wanted you spared. A parent, a grandmother, someone who loved you and had learned the hard way what it costs to show too much. And some of it you forged yourself, in a season when there was no net beneath you and failing was not something you could afford. Either way, it was not paranoia. It was a reasonable answer to real danger.

That is the part worth saying plainly before any of it goes on the stand: the armor worked. Keeping your face still when you were terrified, moving so no one saw you coming, holding your power quietly until the moment it was needed, treating what you knew as the one inheritance no one could take, refusing to fail because failing meant going under. These were not flaws. They were skills, and some of them may have saved you.

But every piece of armor has a second life. First it protects you. Then, if you wear it long enough, it begins to shape you. The stillness that once hid your fear becomes a face you can no longer take off. The vow never to fail hardens into a cage with no door. You stop noticing you have it on, because by now it feels like your own skin.

The question in this count is not whether the armor was necessary. It almost certainly was. The question is quieter and harder. Are you still defending yourself in rooms where the fight is already over?

So carry this question through this count:

THE QUESTION BEFORE YOU

When you reach for the armor now, is it answering a real threat, or only the memory of one?

THE FOURTH WITNESS

“Never let them see you sweat.”

DIRECT EXAMINATION

This one is armor, and it was probably handed to you by someone who loved you and was trying to keep you safe. It promises power through composure. If no one sees your fear, or the strain it took to get here, then you look untouchable, and untouchable people seem harder to attack. For anyone who learned early that visible weakness gets punished, who had to be twice as prepared to be taken half as seriously, this is not a style tip. It is survival. And it works. Calm hands at the table really do command the room. A face that gives nothing away really does keep the other side from learning where you are soft.

I have spent a career inside this one. As a lawyer I learned fast that a room reads any visible strain as a crack to push on, so I kept my face still and my hands steady no matter what the day had cost me. And as the one in charge, I carried it further: I did not let the people who work for me see that I was having a hard day, because I decided long ago that their footing depended on mine looking solid.

So the strength you feel in the line is earned. There are places where the sweat would have cost you everything, and you were right to hide it.

But notice if, under the pride, there is also something tired. The exhaustion of a person who has not been able to set the armor down in a very long time. That tiredness is information too.

CROSS-EXAMINATION

The line makes an assumption it never says out loud: that the sweat is shameful. That struggle must be hidden, and that letting another person see your fear is always weakness.

And it quietly folds two very different instructions into one. Don't show your soft spots to someone who would use them against you, which is often wise. And don't show your humanity to anyone, ever, which is corrosive. The first is reading a threat. The second is a sentence you serve on yourself.

Because armor you cannot take off is not protection anymore. It is a cell. If no one is ever permitted to see you sweat, then no one is permitted to see you at all, and you have kept the people who love you at the exact same distance as the people who would harm you. They cannot help with a struggle they are not allowed to know about. And hiding the sweat does not stop the sweating. It only means you do it alone, at night, where no one can reach you. The composure is real on the outside and very expensive on the inside, and the bill comes due in a body that never got to rest and relationships that never got to be close.

There is one more cost, and it is the quietest. A child watching you never sweat learns that this is what strength looks like, picks up the same armor, and hands it down to their own children, who were never there for whatever made it necessary in the first place.

None of this makes the line false. Some places really do require the mask. What it forgets is that not every room is that room.

A fuller, messier truth

There are places where you should never let them see you sweat, and whoever taught you this was right about them. The negotiation, the table where showing fear gets you eaten. But a person who treats every encounter as enemy territory spends an entire life in armor. The real skill was always knowing which is which. The part that may never have been taught to you is that some rooms are safe enough, and in those the brave thing, the genuinely strong thing, is to let someone see you sweat.

FEEL. PAUSE. ACT.

FEEL. Notice whether the line brought up pride or fatigue. If it was fatigue, sit with it, because that is the weight of armor you have worn so long you forgot it was a choice.

PAUSE. Ask the question the saying never lets you ask. Which room am I actually in? Is the person in front of me a threat I need to armor against, or someone safe I am armoring against out of pure habit?

ACT. Pick one person who has genuinely earned it, and let them see one true thing you would normally hide. Say "I'm scared about this," or "I could use some help with this," out loud, once. If you lead people, the small version can sound like this: "I can be steady for the people I lead without pretending I am never tired." Keep it small. You are not tearing the armor off for good. You are taking it off for one sentence in one safe room, and noticing that the ceiling does not fall in when you do.

§

Which spaces are safe is yours to judge. You have spent your whole life reading rooms, and you are good at it. The thing to watch for is the moment you start treating every single one as enemy territory. When that happens, the armor has stopped protecting a life and started replacing it.

THE FIFTH WITNESS

"They should never see you coming."

DIRECT EXAMINATION

This is the wisdom of the underestimated, and if it was handed to you, it was probably handed to you by someone who had been underestimated their whole life and learned to make it pay. The logic is sharp. If they don't see you coming, they don't block the door, don't prepare a defense against a person they never noticed. You let them think less of you, and you arrive already won. Being counted out becomes a tactical gift, and there is a real, quiet pleasure in it, the satisfaction of the operator who lets the room misjudge them and says nothing.

This was one of my mother's favorite mantras. No matter how far I got, she would say, let them underestimate you; better to be counted out than to be seen coming. She had spent a lifetime being underestimated and had made it work for her, and she was handing me the same edge.

I built a career on exactly that. For close to forty years I have owned or run my own firm, and for most of them the peers I went out with had no idea I was the one running it. One evening, working late, I had a process server drop off documents and take me for the cleaning person, and I let the mistake stand. By then, being underestimated sat closer to cover than to insult.

So the satisfaction is earned. For people who were never handed power and had to take it sideways, surprise is sometimes the only door anyone ever left open.

But notice if, under the satisfaction, there is also a kind of solitude. The particular loneliness of being the only one who knows the plan.

CROSS-EXAMINATION

The line assumes that being unseen is always the advantage, and that being seen is always the risk.

Hold that up to the light. Surprise is a tactic. It is a brilliant one, in the right contest, against an actual opponent. But a person who makes it a way of living pays a strange price. If no one ever sees you coming, then in time no one sees you at all. They see your finished wins and never the person who wanted them. You become known by your outcomes and unknown as yourself, and those are not the same thing.

There is the loneliness too. A plan you can never reveal is a plan you carry alone, and a life of never being seen coming is a life permanently braced, always running the long game, never once able to walk in openly and simply be met. Being underestimated by your enemies is leverage. Being unknown to your own people is a cost you stopped noticing you were paying. The people who love you cannot celebrate a dream they were never allowed to know you had.

The line holds, as far as it goes. There are contests you win precisely by being unseen. What it never tells you is when the game is over and you are allowed to be visible again.

A fuller, messier truth

There are arenas where they should never see you coming, and the surprise really is your edge, and you were smart to use it. But surprise was always a tactic, not an address. A person no one ever sees coming is also a person no one ever truly sees. Stay invisible in the rooms you have to win that way. But somewhere, with someone, let yourself be seen arriving, on purpose, as exactly who you are. Being underestimated is a weapon. It was never meant to be a home.

FEEL. PAUSE. ACT.

FEEL. Go back to whichever it was, the operator's quiet satisfaction or the solitude underneath it. If it was the solitude, that is the part of you grown tired of winning in rooms where no one knows your name.

PAUSE. Ask the question the saying never asks. Am I keeping this hidden because revealing it would actually cost me something here, or out of pure habit? Do I want to win this one unseen, or do I, for once, want to be seen?

ACT. Choose one person who is genuinely on your side, and let them see you coming. Tell them a plan or a hope while it is still unfinished and you could still fail in front of them. "Here's what I'm trying to do, and I don't know yet if I can pull it off."

Or, more exposed still, "I want this, and I'm telling you before I know how it ends." Not the polished win you reveal once it is safe, but the wanting, out loud, before the outcome is known. You are practicing letting someone in on the move before the move is won.

§

When to show your hand is your call; you are a better strategist than I am. But mind the day you start hiding it even from the people who are holding cards for you. That is the cost arriving, right on schedule, exactly as quietly as you taught it to.

THE SIXTH WITNESS

"Walk softly but carry a big stick."

DIRECT EXAMINATION

Most people know this as Roosevelt's line, and his word was speak. Walk is the version that got handed to you, and the change matters, because walking softly is about more than how you talk. It is how you move through the whole world. Quietly, without announcing yourself, drawing no fire, while the power stays ready behind you in case you ever need it.

And there is real wisdom in it. The loudest person in the room is almost never the most powerful one. Bluster is what people reach for when they do not actually have the stick. To move quietly while genuinely carrying weight is a grounded authority that noise can never buy, and if you were taught to keep your head down and still be formidable, this line is the elegant resolution of those two orders. Be soft on the surface. Be unanswerable underneath. The calm it gives you is real.

This one came from my mother too, and her word was *walk*. For me, the stick was my legal skill, my credentials, and the power and money that came with them. For a long stretch I carried all of it everywhere, because it was what kept me from being pushed. What I notice now is how rarely I need to reach for it. Most of the time, no one across from me is trying to take anything, and the day is not a contest I have to win. There is nothing left to brace against.

But notice whether the calm comes with a weight you have stopped feeling, the way you stop feeling a bag you have carried so long it has become part of your shoulder.

CROSS-EXAMINATION

The line assumes you should always be carrying the stick. That the soft walk is only safe because of the force held in reserve, so the force must always be there, always ready.

Run that out to its end. A person who always carries the big stick is a person always prepared for a fight, including in all the years and settings where no fight is coming. The stick is heavy, and if you can never set it down, you are braced for a war that peacetime keeps failing to deliver. You lose the ability to be in a room that needs no stick at all, because you have forgotten how to walk without one.

And the soft walk has its own way of going wrong. Walking softly as a strategy can quietly become walking softly as a habit, until you are not moving with controlled power, you are just making yourself small and letting yourself go unheard, and calling it strength. Worse, a person always holding the stick relates to the whole world through leverage. Every exchange carries a quiet calculation of force, and you cannot be tender with someone while your hand is on a weapon, even a weapon you would never use on them. Even people who love you can begin to feel like opposing counsel when you have forgotten how to be unarmed.

My mother was not wrong. Quiet power is genuine power, and she was teaching me to be formidable without becoming a target. She just never mentioned that the stick is allowed to be set down. Setting it down does not mean you no longer have it. It means you no longer have to prove, in every room, that it is within reach.

A fuller, messier truth

Walking softly with strength in reserve is real wisdom, and the point of carrying a big stick was always so that you would not have to swing it. But a stick you can never put down stops being a tool and becomes a tax you pay on every step, and a person who is always armed cannot be soft with anyone, including the people who would never make them fight. The strength was in having the stick. The freedom is in knowing it can lean against the wall while you sit down.

FEEL. PAUSE. ACT.

FEEL. Notice whether the line gives you that grounded, quiet-power feeling, or whether what surfaces is the tiredness of never once being unarmed. The tiredness is the weight reporting in.

PAUSE. Ask what the saying leaves out. Am I carrying the stick because this room genuinely calls for it, or out of a vigilance I have never been able to switch off? When did I last walk in somewhere and leave it at the door?

ACT. Pick one safe, low-stakes moment and walk in without the stick. That means dropping the readiness to defend and the quiet calculation of who has the upper hand, and simply being present and a little soft for one conversation. Go into a lunch without rehearsing how you'll handle it if it turns on you.

Or let yourself want something openly, with no fallback plan held in reserve. Ask for the thing you actually want, and don't have a backup ready for when they say no. You are leaning the stick against the wall for a single conversation, and noticing things stay safe without it.

§

You have read terrain your whole life, often better than you give yourself credit for, so where you can disarm is yours to call. Just look at whether you have begun carrying the stick into rooms full of people who love you. That weight is the one you are allowed to put down first.

THE SEVENTH WITNESS

"My education is my trust fund."

● DIRECT EXAMINATION

For a lot of people this is not a saying at all. It is a survival strategy that happened to fit into one sentence. If you were not handed money or land or a name that opened doors, then the one inheritance available to you was the one you could build inside your own head. And unlike money, it feels like the one thing no one can take. It does not vanish in a market crash, and it crosses every border you will ever cross. For anyone who started with nothing, this line is not a platitude. It is the literal thing that got them out, and they are right to be proud of it.

This one was not a saying in my house. It was the plan. There was no money to inherit, no land, no name that opened a door. What my family could give me, they gave: they made sure I was educated, and that education was the one thing that ever paid us back.

And it is truer than almost any other saying in this book. Knowledge really is a form of capital, and it really is uniquely yours. So the pride you feel reading it is not a trick of the ego. It is earned, possibly across a lifetime, possibly across generations.

But notice if, riding alongside the pride, there is also a low and constant pressure. The sense that you must always be the one who knows, and that being caught not knowing would cost you something you cannot afford to lose.

CROSS-EXAMINATION

Here the cross-examination has to be gentle, because the line is mostly right. The gap is not in the value of the education. It is hidden in the words trust fund.

A trust fund is security. It is a hedge, a wall against scarcity, a thing you accumulate so that you will never be vulnerable again. And that framing quietly tells you what your education is for: protection. But protection was never the whole of what learning offered. A real education was also supposed to open you, to make you curious and a little more alive, and if you only ever treat it as insurance, you can take a thing built to enlarge your life and shrink it into a fortress around it.

There is a second catch in the phrase. A trust fund is finished capital. You bank it, and then you live off it. But an education is never banked. The person who treats a degree as a completed trust fund stops learning the day they collect it, and spends the rest of their life defending what they already know rather than staying open to what they don't.

And here is the cost that links this saying back to the others in this count. If your security is your knowing, then not knowing becomes a threat to your very safety. You cannot say "I don't know." You cannot be a beginner, cannot walk into a room as the least informed person in it, because your whole net worth is staked on being the one who knows. It is the same armor as never letting them see you sweat, only worn on the inside. Never let them see you not know.

The line is almost entirely right. Your education is a trust fund, maybe the only one you were ever going to get. It misses one thing: a door can be quietly rebuilt into a wall.

A fuller, messier truth

Your education really is a trust fund, the one inheritance no one can take from you, and whoever taught you this was likely right about the world they were preparing you to survive. But a trust fund is something you live off, and an education is something you live in. Treat it only as security and you turn a door into a wall. It was meant to make you harder to dismiss, yes, and also more curious, and more able to say "I don't know" without feeling your worth drop a single point. The richest version of you is not the one who banked the most. It is the one who never stopped spending it on curiosity.

FEEL. PAUSE. ACT.

FEEL. Notice whether the line brought up clean pride, or pride with a pressure under it. If there was pressure, that is the part of you that has been standing guard over the vault, exhausted, certain that the moment you are caught not knowing, something terrible happens.

PAUSE. Ask the questions the saying does not. Did I learn all of this to be safe, or to be free? Is my competence a tool I pick up, or a wall I stand behind? And when did I last learn something completely useless, purely because it delighted me?

ACT. Two options, and both will feel slightly unsafe, which is how you know they matter. Learn one thing this month with no use and no credential attached, something you will be genuinely bad at, and let yourself be a visible beginner. Take a class, try a hobby, or ask a question you are afraid someone thinks you should already know. Or, in a room where you would normally cover, say "I don't know" out loud, once, and watch your worth survive it intact. You are practicing spending the trust fund on curiosity instead of only standing guard over it.

§

Whether you have turned your learning into armor is not mine to say. Only you know whether "I don't know" leaves your mouth as plain honesty or as exposure. But how those three words feel when you say them is the tell, and it has been waiting for you to notice.

THE EIGHTH WITNESS

"Failure is not an option."

DIRECT EXAMINATION

For most people this is a motivational line, the kind of thing stitched on a pillow or shouted in a locker room. For the immigrant it is something else entirely. It is not motivation. It is a description of the actual conditions.

When you arrive in a new country with nothing, failure is not an option because there is no option to fail into. There is no family money waiting to catch you, no plan to move back in with your parents and regroup, because your parents are an ocean away and going back would feel like making the whole crossing, the whole sacrifice that got you onto the plane, mean nothing. So the person who picks you up at the airport does not tell you to follow your dreams. They tell you the truth.

He met me at the airport with the kind of face people wear when they are happy to see you and already calculating what the world will require of you. I had my bags, my accent, my hope, and no real idea yet what it meant to have crossed into a life where no one owed me a soft landing.

He did not give me a speech about dreams. He did not say this would be easy. He said, in whatever words he used that day, you cannot fail here. You have no safety net here.

And I understood him. Not as pressure, though it was pressure. Not as cruelty, because it was not cruelty. I understood it as weather. As fact. As the rule of the place I had just entered.

He was handing me the only piece of armor the situation actually called for. So the resolve you feel reading this line is not borrowed. It is the spine that carried you across, and it works. It summons everything you have and allows no diluting plan B. For a great many people, this exact sentence is the reason they are standing where they stand.

CROSS-EXAMINATION

The cross-examination here has to be careful, because the line was often simply true. For the crossing, failure really was not an option, and whoever told you so was describing the world accurately.

The trouble is what happens when the rule outlives the emergency. When you go on applying a mission-critical standard to an ordinary life, years and decades after the crossing, in rooms where the stakes are no longer survival.

Because failure is not only an option. It is the curriculum. It is how every hard thing gets learned. A person who is never allowed to fail quietly stops attempting anything they cannot already guarantee. They play only the games they know they can win, and they feel every ordinary setback as a catastrophe, a verdict on their worth, the floor giving way beneath them. The mantra that was supposed to make you unstoppable can make you brittle and small instead, because it walls you off from the exact failures that growth is made of. The people who actually do the most fail constantly. They have just made failing cheap and survivable, rather than forbidden.

And here is the quiet cost. If failure is never permitted, then when it comes anyway, and it will, because no one alive goes undefeated, it arrives as shame instead of as information. You hide it. You cannot learn from a thing you are too ashamed to look at. So the rule that was meant to guarantee your success ends up robbing you of the one thing failure was always there to give.

The line was often simply true. There are crossings where failure truly is not an option. What it leaves out is that you have arrived, and that the far shore runs by different rules than the water did.

A fuller, messier truth

There are moments where failure is not an option, and your crossing may well have been one of them, and the person who told you so was telling you the truth about the world you had just landed in. But that rule was for the crossing, not for the whole of the life on the other side.

Once you are safe, failure stops being the enemy and becomes the curriculum. The people who build the most are not the ones with no failures behind them. They are the ones who made failing survivable enough that they could afford to attempt the things that mattered. The aim was never a life with no failure in it. It was a life large enough to hold some.

FEEL. PAUSE. ACT.

FEEL. Notice the resolve the line gives you, the straightening of the spine, because that is real and it earned its place. But notice too if there is a dread underneath it, the low hum of a person who has not been allowed to rest, who believes that a single failure would be the end of them.

PAUSE. Ask the question the rule will not let you ask. Is this genuinely a moment where failure is not an option, or am I treating ordinary life like the crossing it no longer is? And what have I never even attempted, because I could not promise myself I would win?

ACT. Do one thing this week that you might be bad at, on purpose, somewhere the only thing at risk is your pride. If failing feels especially dangerous to you, start as small as letting yourself be visibly new at something that does not threaten your livelihood. Sign up for the class, or send the draft you have been polishing so long it has become a hiding place. Or take one old failure you have been carrying as shame, and write down in a single sentence what it taught you, which turns it from a verdict back into a lesson. You are practicing spending a small, survivable failure and noticing the floor holds.

§

Sorting the crossing from ordinary life is something only you can do; you read the stakes the day you landed, and you can read them now. But notice if you have been treating every attempt as if the whole journey rode on it. It means the rule has outlived the emergency that made it true.

What Armor Am I Still Wearing?

You came up through rooms that asked you to harden. Before the next count, look squarely at what you are still carrying out of them.

Which piece of armor did you recognize as your own before you finished the sentence?

Where are you still braced against a threat that ended years ago?

What do you fear would happen if you set one piece down, and is that danger real now, or only remembered?

The armor was not a mistake. It may have saved you. That still does not mean it is keeping you safe today.

THE RULING

*The ruling is **yours.***

JURY ROOM

Use the space below to respond to the deliberation questions, record what surfaced, or put your ruling into words.

IN THE COURT OF CLARITY

COUNT THREE

THE PEOPLE,	CASE NO. 606692
Plaintiff,	JUDGE: YOU
v.	
THE INNER VOICES YOU WERE TOLD TO TRUST,	
Defendant.	

The charge: **that they crowned one inner voice and silenced the rest.**

Heart, Gut, and Mind

WITNESSES IN THIS COUNT

The first two counts began with what came from outside you: the bonds that shaped you, and the rooms you had to survive. This count turns inward, to the voices that feel like they belong to you alone: the heart that swears it knows, the gut that insists, the mind that calmly builds its case. At one time or another, you have been told to trust each of them completely.

The trouble is that they disagree, and each one speaks with total confidence while it does. Your heart pulls you toward someone your gut distrusts. Your gut recoils from a thing your mind can justify perfectly. Your mind builds a clean case for a choice that leaves your body hollow. If any single one of them were truly the final authority, you would not feel torn so often. You would simply obey it and be right.

So here is the distinction this count is built on, and it sits near the center of the whole book: these three are witnesses. They are not the judge. Each one carries real information, sometimes the kind you could get no other way, and each one is also capable of misleading you with a straight face. A feeling is evidence. It is not a verdict. A thought is evidence too. It is not the court.

The work is not to pick one voice and crown it. The work is to put each on the stand and tell the part that knows something from the part that is only insisting.

This count ends on the voice we most often trust to rule: the thinking mind. It puts the hardest version of the question to that voice, because the mind is the one most likely to believe it is not a witness at all, but the court itself.

So carry this question through this count:

THE QUESTION BEFORE YOU

When an inner voice speaks with total certainty, is it handing you evidence, or a verdict it has not earned the right to give?

THE NINTH WITNESS

"Follow your heart."

DIRECT EXAMINATION

This one is permission, and for a lot of us it arrives like air after a long time underwater. If you were raised to be practical, to want less, to do the sensible thing and quiet the part of you that wanted more, then "follow your heart" is a door swinging open. It says your desire is allowed. Your love matters. The pull you feel toward a person, a place, a life that makes no sense on paper is not a flaw to be corrected. It is a compass to be trusted.

And the heart really does know things. It knows the job that looks perfect on paper and feels like a slow death. It knows the person who makes no logical sense and somehow feels like home. There are truths the heart reaches years before the mind will admit them, so the hope you feel reading this line is not naive. The heart is a real instrument of knowledge, and a life that never consults it is a life half-lived.

But notice, under the hope, whether there is also a small hesitation. Some part of you that has followed its heart before and has the scars to show for it.

Look at the verb. Not consult your heart, not listen to your heart, but follow it. Obey it. Let it lead. That one word quietly turns the heart from a voice in the room into the one who gives the orders.

Here is the trouble. The heart is a magnificent witness and a terrible judge. It hands you real, urgent, vital information, and it hands you all of it at once, with no sense of proportion and no memory. It does not recall that last spring it was just as certain about something that nearly wrecked you. On its own it cannot tell love from hunger, or destiny from dopamine. It will mistake the tug of an old wound for the pull of a real future, because the wound feels like home, being the shape of your first heartbreak. Following the heart blindly has ruined as many lives as ignoring it ever did, and if you are honest, you have a story of your own filed under each.

And this is the saying that sits closest to the nerve of this whole book, so I want to be exact. Everything in these pages argues that the feeling is the first data, the signal you must never put on mute. "Follow your heart" agrees that the heart matters, and then makes one fatal move. It promotes the witness to judge. The feeling was meant to open the inquiry, not end it. A court that let a single passionate witness deliver the verdict would not be a court at all.

The line isn't lying to you. Your heart belongs at the center of the decision. It was just never meant to make the decision alone.

A fuller, messier truth

Your heart is one of the truest witnesses you have, and you should never put it on mute, because it knows things your reasoning will keep denying for years. But a witness is not a verdict. Let your heart testify in full, and then let the rest of you cross-examine it, your hard-won memory of where this certainty led the last time, and the people who love you and have no reason to lie. The heart was never built to drive the car alone. It was built to tell you, loudly and honestly, where you actually want to go. Then you, the whole of you, decide whether to go there.

FEEL. PAUSE. ACT.

FEEL. Let the heart speak first, and let it have its full say, before you reach for the sensible voice that wants to cut it off. Notice the surge of yes. Notice, too, if there is an older caution underneath it. You are not choosing between them yet. You are letting both testify.

PAUSE. Ask the question that separates a witness from a verdict. Is this my heart's wisdom, or my heart's hunger? Wisdom may sound like a quiet, steady knowing. Hunger often arrives as urgency, as if the thing must happen now or disappear forever. Have I felt exactly this certainty before, and where did it take me? And what does the rest of me, the part that remembers, have to say?

ACT. The next time your heart is sure about something that matters, give it the full hearing it deserves, and then put it through one honest cross-examination before you move. Ask it out loud: have I been this certain before, and how did that end? Then sit with the answer for one night, not to talk yourself out of the heart, but to let the whole of you into the room. Use the night to see whether the wanting is still true when urgency has had time to settle. In the morning, decide. You are practicing letting the heart testify without letting it rule.

§

Whether to follow this particular heart is not mine to say, because from here I cannot tell your wisdom from your hunger. But you can, if you let the feeling finish speaking and then ask it one true question. The verdict was always yours. The heart simply gets to go first.

THE TENTH WITNESS

"Trust your gut."

DIRECT EXAMINATION

This one feels like coming home to yourself. It says the fast, wordless read you get on a person or a situation, the one you cannot explain and did not reason your way to, is real knowledge and worth heeding. The hair lifting on your neck. The quiet no in your stomach before the meeting has even started. The two-second call that turned out right while everyone who deliberated for a week got it wrong.

And there is genuine truth in it. Your gut is a high-speed processor. Beneath conscious thought, your mind is reading thousands of tiny signals and handing you the read as a sensation, and when that machinery has been trained on real experience, it is often faster and wiser than the slow, talky part of you. The seasoned nurse who senses a patient is crashing before the monitors agree. The negotiator whose stomach drops at a number that looked fine on paper. This is not mysticism. It is expertise moving faster than language. And about danger especially, the gut is one of the oldest and most reliable instruments you own.

So the confidence you feel reading this line is often earned. The trouble is that it feels exactly as earned when it isn't.

Here is the catch the saying never mentions. The gut is a pattern-matcher, and it is only ever as good as the patterns it was trained on.

The same fast, certain jolt that correctly tells the nurse a patient is crashing also fires when you meet someone whose face or manner happens to match an old fear or an inherited prejudice. And here is the part that should stop you. From the inside, those two feel identical. Trained wisdom and raw bias arrive in the exact same envelope, a wordless certainty with no return address. The gut never shows its work. That is precisely what makes it fast, and precisely why it cannot be trusted blindly.

Because a gut trained on a thousand real encounters is wisdom, and a gut trained on one old wound is just that wound, firing on cue and dressed up as instinct. The quiet prejudices you absorbed from the place you grew up speak in that very same calm voice. The saying tells you to obey all of it without once asking which one is talking. If your gut tightens because someone's story keeps changing, that may be information. If it tightens because this person reminds you of someone who once hurt you, that may be memory.

This is the cousin of the chapter before it, and the difference is worth holding. The heart oversteps by wanting to be the judge. The gut oversteps in a sneakier way. It hides its evidence. It is a witness who refuses to say how they came to know what they claim to know, and a witness like that can be your most seasoned expert or your most frightened child, and the two sound exactly alike on the stand.

The line points at something real. Your gut is knowledge, and about danger you should heed it fast. What it cannot do, on its own, is tell you whether it learned what it knows from experience or from fear.

A fuller, messier truth

Trust your gut, and then ask it the one question it will never volunteer: where did you learn this? When the read is about danger, act first and audit later, because that is the one arena where the cost of being slow is too high. But when it is a snap judgment about a person or a path, make the certainty show its papers before you let it decide. A gut schooled on real experience is faster than your reasoning and worth following. A gut schooled on fear is only fear that learned to sound sure. The feeling is the same. The schooling is everything.

FEEL. PAUSE. ACT.

FEEL. Honor the jolt. The drop in the stomach, the wordless yes or no, is real information, and your first job is to notice it rather than talk yourself out of it on principle.

PAUSE. Then ask your gut the thing it cannot say unprompted. Where did you go to school on this? Is it trained on real, relevant experience with exactly this kind of situation, or is it matching to an old pattern, a fear or a face from long ago, that may have nothing to do with what is in front of me now?

ACT. The next time your gut hands you a strong read on a person, finish this sentence out loud before you act on it: "My gut is reacting to ___." If the blank fills with something concrete and relevant, the person dodged three straight questions, the story changed twice, then heed it hard. If the blank fills with something vague, or something that is really about who or what this person reminds you of, slow down and look closer before you move. Danger is the exception. When the gut says leave, leave, and work out the why from somewhere safe.

§

From here I cannot tell whether this particular feeling is your expertise or your echo, so I won't tell you whether to trust it. But you can ask it where it went to school, and how honestly it answers is the tell.

THE ELEVENTH WITNESS

"I think, therefore I am."

DIRECT EXAMINATION

This one arrives with a philosopher's stamp on it, which is part of its power. Descartes went looking for a single thing he could not doubt. He could doubt the world, his senses, even his own body, but the moment he tried to doubt that he was thinking, there was a thinker doing the doubting. So thinking became the floor beneath everything, the one fact that survived.

And we took it home and made it personal. It flatters the part of us we are proudest of. If thinking is the proof that you exist, then your mind is your truest self, and the busy machinery upstairs is not a habit but the very thing that makes you real. For anyone who was the smart one, the one who reasoned their way out of trouble, that is a deeply comfortable idea. When the ground is shaking, at least I still have my mind, and as long as I am thinking, I am still here.

If this line was built to flatter anyone, it was me. I used my mind to get through everything; logic was the instrument I trusted, and feeling was something to suppress, because it got in the way. As an attorney especially, I believed that to stay credible I had to stay logical. For most of my life, that looked like strength.

So watch what the line does to you. For some of us it lands as pride, a quiet yes, my head is my best room. For others it lands as a cage, because if I am my thoughts then I can never put them down. Both reactions are the signal. The pride is worth questioning, and the cage is worth listening to.

CROSS-EXAMINATION

Here is what Descartes actually proved, and what he did not.

He proved that thinking is evidence you exist. He never proved that thinking is the best way to exist, and he certainly never said you are your thoughts. But that is the version that got loose. I think, therefore I am quietly became I am what I think, and from there it became a license to live almost entirely from the neck up.

Look at what that license demotes. Descartes reached his certainty by doubting his body and his senses, setting them aside as unreliable, so the saying we inherited carries that same ranking in its bones. The mind is the real you, and the body, the senses, the wordless animal you also are, all of it ranks lower, suspect, secondary.

Run that belief for thirty years and you get a familiar kind of person. Someone who treats feelings as static to be solved, who cannot fall asleep because the one part of them that proves they exist refuses to stop talking. The over-thinker's prison is built out of this exact sentence. If I stop thinking, do I stop being?

I know this person because I was this person. I did everything the wellness world asks: I ate well, exercised, supplemented, watched my labs. And still my blood pressure climbed, and for a long time I could not see why, because I was looking for a mineral or a medication when a piece I kept missing was permission to feel the thing before I moved past it. My blood pressure sits in a better place now. I am not going to tell you that feeling the thing fixed it, because a number like that has more than one author, and I was working several of them at once. But once I stopped overriding what my body had been trying to say, the rest of it had room to work.

And here is the part that should interest you most, because it is the quiet argument running under this whole book. I think, therefore I am became one of the sentences we used to distrust feeling and rank it beneath thought. But the feeling was the first data. The tightening in your chest when someone said family is everything got you to the question before your reasoning did. The version we inherited put the mind on the throne and the body in the cellar, and most of us have been living in that house ever since.

Thinking is not the false part here. It really is one proof that you exist. It is just far too small a proof, mistaken for the whole.

A fuller, messier truth

You are not only because you think. You are also when you ache, when you are held, when you are so absorbed in a thing that you forget to narrate yourself at all. The mind is a magnificent instrument and a poor master, and some of the realest hours of your life were the ones where the thinking finally went quiet. A baby exists before its first sentence. You did too, and you still do, in every moment you are not explaining.

FEEL. PAUSE. ACT.

FEEL. Notice which one came up, the pride or the cage. If it was pride, ask gently what the pride is guarding, because the head is a very good place to hide from a feeling. If it was the cage, that churn you live inside is the signal itself. The thinking may have become the place you go in order not to feel.

PAUSE. Ask the question the saying steers you away from. When have I felt most alive, and in that moment, was I thinking hard, or had the thinking gone still? Be honest about whether you have been treating your own body and your own feelings as second-class citizens of yourself.

ACT. This one cannot be done by thinking about it, which is the whole point. Today, do one ordinary thing without narrating it. Eat a meal with no phone and no planning of the next thing, and just taste it.

Or, the version that goes deeper: the next time a feeling shows up, instead of analyzing it, find it in your body, where it is sitting and what it weighs, and let it be there for sixty seconds before you let your mind say a single word about it. You are practicing existing without thinking, and noticing that you are still, unmistakably, here.

§

Only you know whether the thinking has become a hiding place; I can't call that from here. But your body keeps a record your reasoning keeps talking over. Where you feel most alive is the evidence, and it has been there the whole time, waiting for you to stop reasoning long enough to read it.

JURY DELIBERATION · COUNT THREE

Which Inner Voice Have I Let Rule?

Three witnesses testified in this count, and each one wanted to be believed completely. Before you go on, weigh how you have been hearing them.

When your heart, your gut, and your mind disagree, which one usually wins, and have you ever asked why it gets the last word?

Where have you treated a feeling as a verdict, or let a thought convince you it was the whole court?

What has the voice you trust least been trying to tell you?

The work was never to crown one of them. It was to remember who does the weighing.

THE RULING

The ruling is ***yours.***

JURY ROOM

Use the space below to respond to the deliberation questions, record what surfaced, or put your ruling into words.

IN THE COURT OF CLARITY

COUNT FOUR

THE PEOPLE,) CASE NO. 606692

Plaintiff,) JUDGE: YOU

v.

THE STORIES YOU WERE HANDED ABOUT PAIN,

Defendant.

The charge: **that they sold you meaning so you would not have to feel.**

Pain and Meaning

WITNESSES IN THIS COUNT

When something breaks you, the sayings arrive almost immediately, often before you have finished understanding what happened. They come from people who love you and cannot bear to watch you hurt, so they are offered as comfort. But listen closely and most of them are doing something quieter than comforting. They are trying to move you past the feeling before you have had the chance to feel it.

Everything happens for a reason hands you a meaning so you do not have to sit in the senselessness. Look on the bright side points you toward the good so you do not have to name the loss. What doesn't kill you makes you stronger reframes the damage as a gift so no one has to call it damage. Time heals all wounds promises that if you simply wait, the work will do itself.

Each of these is reaching toward something true. Meaning can be made from pain, though it is made, not found waiting inside the event. There is often a bright side, and seeing it can keep you upright. Some people do come out of suffering stronger. And time does give a wound room to settle. None of that is the problem.

The problem is what these sayings ask you to skip. They arrive at the precise moment the feeling does, and they offer you a way around it. A reason instead of grief. A bright side instead of anger. Strength instead of damage. Time instead of tending. And feeling, in this book, is not the obstacle. It is the information. A pain you are rushed past is a pain you never get to read.

So this is the most tender part, and it asks the gentlest version of the question.

THE QUESTION BEFORE YOU

When a saying offers to explain your pain, brighten it, redeem it, or wait it out, is it helping you feel what happened, or helping you avoid it?

THE TWELFTH WITNESS

"Everything happens for a reason."

DIRECT EXAMINATION

This may be one of the most comforting sentences we reach for, and it does its best work on the worst days. When something terrible arrives, a death, or a diagnosis no one saw coming, the mind reels not just at the pain but at the randomness. The sense that it could have gone another way, that the universe simply was not paying attention. Into that free fall, "everything happens for a reason" reaches out a hand. It says the pain is not random. There is a design. Something is steering, and your suffering is a chapter in a story that will one day make sense.

And we reach for it because the alternative is almost unbearable. That terrible things sometimes happen for no reason at all, to people who did nothing to deserve them, in a world with no script. The sentence is usually offered out of love, by someone who cannot stand to watch you hurt and wants to hand you something to hold. The comfort it gives is real, and the impulse behind it is kind.

So if this line has gotten you through a night, that is nothing to be ashamed of. Hold onto the comfort for a moment, because we are about to ask what it actually claims.

The sentence makes a quiet and enormous claim. It says the reason exists out there, built into the event, decided in advance. That the loss was aimed at some good.

Hold that up against the worst thing you know of. A child's illness. The cruelty that fell on someone who had only ever been kind. If everything happens for a reason, then some purpose required those things, needed that child to suffer, wrote that devastation into the plan on purpose. Pressed honestly, almost no one actually believes that. The sentence comforts in the abstract and turns monstrous the instant it meets real horror, which is exactly why, said to a freshly grieving person, it can land like a slap. It tells them their loss was meant. That somewhere, on some ledger, it was supposed to happen.

Here is the confusion buried in it. The line quietly fuses two very different things. One is that an event has a built-in purpose, a reason it was sent, which, about genuine suffering, is unprovable and often cruel. The other is that you can make meaning out of what happened, which is true, and powerful, and entirely yours. The saying smuggles the second thing inside the first. It takes your own hard-won, handmade meaning and tells you it was prewired into the tragedy all along.

And believing the strong version costs you. It can trap you in a hunt for the hidden lesson in your own trauma, as though grief came with homework, or tip you into wondering what you did to deserve it. It can also talk you into accepting what should have been fought, because it was meant to be. The sentence that was supposed to comfort you can quietly assign you the job of justifying your own worst day.

The line isn't false in the trivial sense. Things do have causes. That is not the same as saying they have a purpose. Where it goes wrong, and sometimes turns cruel, is in confusing the cause of a thing with the aim behind it, handing you a reason when what you actually have is a choice.

A fuller, messier truth

You cannot always find a reason in what happened. About the worst things, there may be no reason that any decent person would accept. But in time, you may be able to make meaning from it, and that is the part the saying gets backward. The meaning is not waiting inside the event like a prize you have to dig out. It is something you build afterward, with your own hands, out of the wreckage, and the fact that you built it is precisely what makes it real and yours. Not everything happens for a reason. But almost nothing has to stay meaningless, if you are the one who decides to make something of it.

If your faith tells you a reason exists, that belief is yours to hold, and this chapter is not here to take it from you. The harm starts somewhere else: when another person assigns the reason to your loss, or when you force one onto yourself before your grief has had its hearing.

FEEL. PAUSE. ACT.

FEEL. Notice what the line does in you. If it brings comfort, let it, and ask gently what you are reaching for, because that need is honest. And if it brings a flinch, if some part of you was handed this sentence over a real loss and felt it press down rather than lift, that flinch is telling the truth too. You do not have to call your grief a lesson.

PAUSE. Ask the question the sentence skips. Am I being told this happened for a reason, or am I being invited to make meaning from it? Do I have to believe this was meant in order to survive it, or can I let it be senseless and still build something from it with my own hands?

ACT. Take one hard thing you have been trying to find the reason for, and stop searching for the reason it happened. Instead, finish this sentence, on paper: "I do not know if this was meant, but here is what I am going to make of it."

You are trading a hunt that may never end for a choice that is already yours. And if the loss is still fresh, the action is gentler. Let it be senseless for now. Do not let anyone, least of all yourself, rush you toward a tidy meaning before you have had time to feel what you lost.

§

Whether your loss had a reason, I cannot tell you, because I do not know, and anyone who claims to is guessing at the universe. What I can tell you is that the meaning is yours to make, and that you are allowed to make it without first agreeing that the pain was deserved, required, or meant.

THE THIRTEENTH WITNESS

"Look on the bright side."

DIRECT EXAMINATION

This one is hope in five words. When the day has gone dark, it points you toward what is still good, still worth being grateful for, and on the right day that pointing is a lifeline. Rumination is corrosive. Catastrophizing makes a hard thing harder. Deliberately turning your attention toward what is still working is a real skill, and there are mornings when finding the single good thing is the rope that pulls you out of the pit.

So the relief this line offers is not fake. The bright side is a real place, and learning to look at it is one of the more useful things a person can learn. We reach for it, and we hand it to people we love, because watching someone we care about sink is hard, and we want to give them somewhere lighter to stand.

But notice the speed of it. The way it asks you to turn toward the light right now, before you have said a word about the dark.

CROSS-EXAMINATION

Here is the move hidden in the sentence. It does not ask you to also see the good. It asks you to look away from what you are feeling and toward something more pleasant, immediately, before the feeling has had a chance to tell you anything. It treats the feeling as a problem to escape rather than information to read. And that is the exact opposite of everything this book is built on.

Because the feeling you skip does not get left behind. It waits. The grief you brightened past is grief you never finished, and it will return later, often at a worse time. The anger you reframed away does not evaporate, it leaks out sideways, at people who did not earn it. And the fear you refused to sit with was often the one part of you that had spotted a real problem, now talked out of speaking. The dark side is not only pain to be managed. It is frequently the signal itself, the discomfort that is trying to tell you a boundary was crossed, or that something needs to change. Look away too fast and you lose the message along with the ache.

There is a quieter cruelty in it too, on the days someone hands it to you. Told to a person in fresh pain, "look on the bright side" often means something the speaker would never say out loud. Your feelings are uncomfortable for me, please put them away. It teaches you, one cheerful redirection at a time, that your hard feelings are unwelcome, and that the price of company is performing okay.

So the line erases a real difference. Choosing to see the good after you have felt the bad is expansive and healthy. Being ordered to see only the good instead of the bad is a dodge, and sometimes a silencing. Same five words, opposite functions.

The bright side is not the lie here. It is a real place, and worth finding. What the line leaves out is that the light has no back door, and the only way in is straight through the dark.

A fuller, messier truth

The bright side is a real place, and there are days when getting there is what saves you. But it is a destination, not a detour around the feeling, and it only holds your weight if you reached it by walking through the dark side rather than leaping over it. So look on the bright side, yes, but after you have looked, honestly and without hurrying, at the actual one. The order is the whole thing. Let what happened have its hearing first, and then, if you choose, turn toward the light, having already heard what the dark was trying to tell you. The bright side is not false. It is just not first.

FEEL. PAUSE. ACT.

FEEL. Notice the pull toward relief, the wish to skip ahead to the good part. That wish is human and it is not the enemy. But notice what it wants you to step over, the actual feeling waiting underneath, and do not look away from that one just yet.

PAUSE. Ask the question the saying hurries you past. Have I actually felt this, or am I being rushed, by someone else or by my own discomfort, into performing okay? What is this hard feeling trying to tell me before I brighten past it?

ACT. The next time something hurts, give the dark side its hearing before you reach for the light. Say the hard thing in plain words, out loud or on paper, with no "but" and no silver lining stapled to the end of it. Something as plain as "This is hard, and here is exactly why," or "I'm not okay right now," or "What happened actually hurt me."

Stay with it long enough to hear what it is telling you. Then, if you want to, go looking for the bright side, and notice that it lands truer because you earned the way there. And when someone hands you the line mid-grief, you are allowed to answer, "I will get there. I am just not done with this yet."

§

There usually is a bright side to your particular hard thing, and it is usually worth finding, so that is not the question. The question is when, and you do not owe anyone, least of all yourself, a silver lining before you have had time to feel the loss.

THE FOURTEENTH WITNESS

"What doesn't kill you makes you stronger."

DIRECT EXAMINATION

This one is defiance, and there is something magnificent in it. It takes your worst experiences and recasts them as the forge that made you. The scars become evidence that the thing did not get the final word. The thing that should have ended you becomes the thing that tempered you instead. For anyone who has been through something terrible and is still standing, this line offers a way to wear the suffering as armor rather than carry it as damage, and that reframe can feel like getting your power back.

And there is real truth within reach of it. People do come out of hard things changed for the better. They discover they can survive more than they feared, and they walk differently afterward, with a steadiness they did not have before. So the pride you feel saying this line is not vanity. Sometimes it is simply accurate.

But notice if, alongside the pride, there is a quiet strain. The effort of insisting you were strengthened by something that, if you are honest, mostly just hurt.

The trouble is in one small, absolute word: makes. As though strength were the guaranteed output of any pain you happen to survive.

It often is not. A great deal of what does not kill you does not make you stronger. It makes you warier, or smaller. It leaves some people frightened of doors they used to walk through without a thought. Surviving a thing and being improved by it are not the same event, and pretending they are turns into a quiet cruelty, because it implies a corollary nobody says out loud. If you came through your hardship not stronger but diminished, still flinching, still healing, then you must have done it wrong. It is one more way to hand the wounded the blame for their wounds.

And here is what the line gets backward about where strength actually comes from. When people do grow from hardship, and they can, the growth is not delivered by the hardship. The fire alone does not temper you. What tempers you is everything that comes after, the support you found and the slow rebuilding you did. The strength is earned in the recovery, and recovery is not automatic. It depends on things this line never mentions, on whether you had help, whether anyone was there to hold the other end. The saying credits the wound for work the healing did.

This is the danger of believing it too completely. It can talk you into refusing help because you are supposed to be getting tougher, or denying that you are hurt at all because hurt does not fit the story. It can also make endurance look noble in a situation where the wiser move is to get out. At its worst it sends people looking for fires on the theory that they will be forged, when plenty of fires simply burn.

Some of what you survived really did make you stronger, so the line is not simply wrong. Where it fails is in pointing at the wrong thing, thanking the pain for what your recovery actually built.

A fuller, messier truth

Some of what doesn't kill you makes you stronger. Some of it just leaves you tired, or quieter than you used to be, and surviving is not the same as being improved. Pain may reveal strength, but recovery is what builds it. When strength does rise out of a hard thing, it does not rise from the thing itself. It comes from what you did afterward, and who stood with you while you did it. So do not thank the wound. Thank the healing, thank the people who helped you heal, and give yourself the credit for the work. And never go hunting for a fire because you have been told it will forge you. Plenty of fires only burn.

FEEL. PAUSE. ACT.

FEEL. Notice the defiant pride the line gives you, because turning survival into dignity is no small thing and it is yours to keep. But notice too if it is pressuring you to call something strength that mostly just hurt, or to hide the part of you that is still healing. That hidden part is the one telling the truth.

PAUSE. Ask the questions the saying skips. Is this hardship actually making me stronger, or am I being asked to wear my damage as a medal? And the strength I genuinely do have, did the suffering hand it to me, or did I build it afterward, in the part nobody put in the slogan?

ACT. Take one hard thing you have been carrying as the thing that made you stronger, and separate it honestly. What genuinely strengthened me? What simply hurt me and still needs care? Let the part that still needs care stay that way, with no demand that it become a strength on schedule.

Then, for the real strength, name the thing you actually did, or the person who actually helped, that built it, and put the credit there instead of on the wound. If you are in something hard right now, change the question entirely. Stop asking it to make you stronger, and start asking what you need in order to recover from it. Sometimes the honest answer is a way out.

§

I will not be the one to tell you your hardships made you stronger, even though some of them surely did, and that pride is earned. You get to decide which wounds you will call strength and which you will let yourself still be healing from, and you do not owe anyone a story in which the worst thing that ever happened to you was secretly good for you.

THE FIFTEENTH WITNESS

"Time heals all wounds."

DIRECT EXAMINATION

When a loss is fresh, this may be the only sentence that helps. In the worst of it, the pain does not feel like it has an edge, it feels like weather that will never lift, like this is simply how things are now and always will be. Into that, "time heals all wounds" reaches back and says, you will not always feel this way. The intensity is temporary even though it does not feel temporary. And that promise is true. Acute pain really does dull. The thing you cannot imagine surviving on Tuesday is, by some Tuesday far enough away, survivable.

So the comfort here is honest, and the patience it counsels is real wisdom. It tells you not to make permanent decisions inside temporary agony, and to let some time pass before you decide what anything means. On the worst days, the simple promise that the sharpness will fade is a hand reaching back to pull you a few steps forward.

But notice the word doing the heavy lifting, and how little it asks of you: time. As though you could just wait, and be carried to the far shore.

The sentence makes time the healer. You hold still, the clock runs, and the wound closes on its own. And that is not how wounds work, in the body or anywhere else.

Time is not the thing that heals. Time is the condition in which healing can happen, if you tend the wound. The grief you never let yourself feel, the betrayal you filed away unprocessed, none of that closes just because years passed over the top of it. It calcifies. People carry wounds for decades that are not healed at all, only old, and the saying gave them quiet permission to do exactly that, to wait instead of tend, to mistake the passing of time for the doing of work. A wound you only wait out is a wound that may close crooked, or never close at all.

And there is the other word, the absolute one: all. As though every wound, given enough calendar, disappears completely. The deepest ones do not. You do not get over the death of someone you loved, not in the sense the saying implies, where one day it simply stops hurting. What actually happens, when you tend it well and give it years, is gentler and stranger than that. You grow around it. The wound stays roughly its size, and your life slowly grows wider around it, until it is a smaller part of a larger whole. It will still catch you on the anniversary. The song will still take your legs out. And that ache, years on, is not evidence that you failed to heal. It is love that outlived the person it was for, which is the most human thing there is.

So when the wound still hurts long after the saying promised it would not, people conclude something is wrong with them. They are grieving incorrectly. They have not moved on. That is the cruelty hidden in the comfort. It sets a finish line the largest losses were never going to cross, and then lets you believe you are the one who failed to reach it.

Time really is necessary, and fresh pain really does dull, so the line is not false. What it gets wrong is crediting the clock for work only you can do, and promising an erasure the wounds that matter most will never grant.

A fuller, messier truth

Time is the soil. It is not the gardener. Fresh pain dulls with time, so do not rush yourself, but a wound only heals if something tends it, and the tending is yours to do. And the deepest wounds do not vanish even when you tend them beautifully. You do not get over the great losses. You grow around them, slowly, until they sit inside a life grown wide enough to hold them. The wound will still ache on certain days, and that is not failure. That is the shape love takes once it has nowhere left to go.

FEEL. PAUSE. ACT.

FEEL. If you are in fresh pain, let the promise comfort you, because it is true that this sharpness will dull, and you are allowed to lean on that. But if there is an old wound in you that you have been giving time for years, notice whether time has actually been healing it or merely keeping it. The honest answer to that is information.

PAUSE. Ask the questions the saying lets you avoid. Am I healing this, or only waiting it out? Is this a fresh wound that genuinely needs patience, or an old one I have been outlasting instead of tending? And am I waiting for it to disappear, when what it really needs is for me to grow around it?

ACT. If time has passed but the wound still rules the room, it may not need more time. It may need tending. Take one wound you have been giving time, and ask what it actually needs you to do, rather than outlast. Some wounds need to finally be felt, because you skipped the grieving. Some need help you cannot give yourself. Choose one tending act and do it this week, instead of waiting one more year. And for the losses that will never fully close, stop measuring whether the wound is gone, and start noticing whether your life is growing wider around it.

§

No one can tell you how long your healing will take, or whether a given wound will close or become something you carry, and I will not pretend otherwise. But you can tell the difference between healing and waiting, and you are allowed to tend a thing rather than serve out a sentence beside it, hoping the clock does what only care can.

What Have I Been Asked to Call Healing?

This count asked you to slow down where the world usually hurries you along. Stay here a moment longer before you move on.

Which of these comforts were you handed at the very moment you most needed to simply feel?

Where have you called something healed because waiting was easier than tending it?

What feeling have you been talking yourself out of, and what might it be trying to show you?

You are allowed to feel the thing before you make sense of it.

THE RULING

*The ruling is **yours.***

JURY ROOM

Use the space below to respond to the deliberation questions, record what surfaced, or put your ruling into words.

IN THE COURT OF CLARITY

COUNT FIVE

THE PEOPLE, Plaintiff,

v.

THE SAYINGS THAT PUSHED YOU TO ACT, Defendant.

CASE NO. 606692

JUDGE: YOU

The charge: **that they dressed motion up as wisdom.**

Ambition, Action, and Creation

WITNESSES IN THIS COUNT

The sayings ahead are the ones that get you out of the chair. They are about motion: trying, persisting, risking, building, speaking the life you want into being. After a count about feeling, that is bracing, and it should be. Nothing in this book argues for staying still. A life is built by doing, and these sayings are right that doing is where a life changes.

So this count honors action. What it questions is the assumption hidden inside each of these sayings: that the doing is the whole of the wisdom.

Each saying blurs a different line. Never give up blurs persistence with discernment, and never asks whether the thing you refuse to quit is worth what it is taking from you. Knowledge is power blurs knowing with doing, as if knowledge that never turns into action were anything more than weight you carry. You miss 100% of the shots you don't take blurs courage with shot-taking, weighing only the shots you skipped and saying nothing about the reckless ones that cost too much. The best way to predict the future is to create it blurs influence with control, handing you authorship over outcomes you only ever partly shape. As I speak, so I create blurs naming with making, promising the words will do the work, as if saying a thing were the same as building it.

What they share is a blind spot about discernment. They make motion a virtue in itself and quietly drop the harder questions: whether this is the right thing to do, whether this is the right time to do it, and whether it is actually working or only moving.

Pain can make agency feel small. But you do have real agency: more than helplessness admits, and less than these sayings sometimes promise. You author your efforts, not your outcomes, and most of these sayings smudge that line, handing you full credit and full blame for results that were never entirely yours.

This count is about that line: between the motion you control and the result you do not.

So carry this question through this count:

THE QUESTION BEFORE YOU

When a saying urges you to act, is it pointing you toward something worth doing, or only flattering you for moving at all?

THE SIXTEENTH WITNESS

"Never give up."

DIRECT EXAMINATION

This one is pure fuel. Every comeback you have ever admired runs on it. The overnight success that actually took eleven years. The dream that survived only because its owner refused to put it down when putting it down would have been so easy and so reasonable. "Never give up" promises that the difference between the people who make it and the people who don't is not luck or talent but stamina, and there is hard truth in that. Most people quit in the difficult middle, a step or two before the thing would have finally turned, and the ones who keep walking get what the quitters left on the table.

And it hands you back the one thing despair tries to steal, control. You cannot guarantee the outcome, but you can decide whether you stop, and on the days when that is the only choice still in your hands, it is a powerful one. For anyone who has been underestimated, "never give up" is not a slogan. It is the engine.

So the determination you feel reading it is well placed. The trouble is hiding in the first word, the absolute one.

Start with that word, never, and how total it is. As though stopping were always the wrong move, and persistence always the right one.

But knowing when to stop is a skill, and it may be a harder and braver one than knowing how to continue. Sometimes the goal is wrong. The relationship will not change no matter how faithfully you keep showing up. The career is a slow erosion of the person you meant to be. The project should have been buried two years ago.

Persisting on the wrong thing is not grit. It is the sunk cost fallacy wearing grit's jacket, and "I have come too far to quit now" has kept people in dead marriages and whole lives that were never theirs, long past the point where staying made any sense at all.

Here is the cost the word hides. Every hour you spend refusing to quit the wrong thing is an hour stolen from the right one. Persistence has an opportunity cost, and "never give up" makes you blind to it, because it only ever teaches you one of the two moves a life actually requires. You learn to push. You never learn to fold a losing hand and carry what is left of your chips to a better table.

Of all these, this is the one that never took hold in me. I always knew when to stop: if something was not working after a fair try, I let it go, and I never once felt that as giving up. Forty years of building one firm taught me the other half too, that some things are worth holding well past the point of comfort. The skill was never persistence or quitting on its own. It was knowing which one a thing actually called for.

And there is the shame. Because the saying frames quitting as weakness, as a flaw in your character, people cannot make the wise stop when they need it most. They would rather drown slowly than wear the word quitter, so they stay, and call the staying strength. The mantra meant to empower you quietly removes one of your essential moves and tells you that reaching for it would make you a coward.

Persistence, when the thing is right, is some of the best advice there is, so the line is not the problem. The problem is the word never, which treats refusing to quit as the whole skill. The real one was always telling a thing that is hard because it is worth it from a thing that is hard because it is wrong.

A fuller, messier truth

Persistence is a superpower, and most people really do quit a step before the turn, so when the goal is right, never give up is close to gospel. But never is a lie, because the wisest and bravest thing you ever do might be to stop. The skill the saying refuses to teach is the hard one, telling the difference between hard-because-it-is-worth-it and hard-because-it-is-wrong. Hard-and-right may tire you, but it still points toward a life you want. Hard-and-wrong drains you while asking you to call the draining devotion. Push through the first with everything you have. Walk away from the second without calling it failure. Quitting the wrong thing is not giving up. It is giving the right thing your life back.

FEEL. PAUSE. ACT.

FEEL. Notice the determination the line lights in you, because that fire is real and you will need it. But then feel for which thing is under your urge to quit. There is the clean fatigue of work that is hard because it matters, and there is the heavier dread of being somewhere you were never meant to stay. They feel different in the body, and that difference is your first piece of evidence.

PAUSE. Ask the questions the word forbids. Is this hard because it is worth it, or hard because it is wrong? Am I still moving toward something I want, or only refusing to stop because stopping feels like losing? And what would I choose if "quitter" were not a word I was afraid of?

ACT. Take the thing you have been gritting your teeth through, and run one honest test on it. If I had not already poured years and money into this, would I choose to start it today, knowing what I now know? If the answer is no, then it is not persistence keeping you there. It is the fear of quitting.

So make the braver move. Give yourself explicit permission to stop one wrong thing, deliberately, naming it out loud as a wise stop rather than a defeat. And if the thing is genuinely right, do the opposite on purpose. Recommit, and call the difficulty what it is, the price you have chosen to pay.

§

Which one your thing is, hard-and-right or hard-and-wrong, only you can finally weigh, so the call to stay or walk is yours. But you have both moves, and you always did. Walking away from the wrong thing was never the failure the word made it out to be.

THE SEVENTEENTH WITNESS

"Knowledge is power."

● DIRECT EXAMINATION

This one is a promise of fairness in a usually unfair world. It says power is not only inherited or bought, it can be earned, by anyone willing to learn. The library is one of the few rooms that even tries to open to the heir and the orphan on something like equal terms. So if you started with nothing, the prepared mind becomes the great equalizer, the way you out-maneuver people who were handed everything except the willingness to study. For the self-taught, the one who read their way out, this line is not abstract. It is a door, and it opens for effort rather than for pedigree.

And there is real truth in it. The informed patient who walks into the appointment having done the reading often gets different care. The person who knows their rights and the actual numbers is harder to push around. Information asymmetry is genuine leverage, and closing the gap between what you know and what the powerful know is one of the truest forms of self-defense there is.

In one place above all I have always treated knowledge this way, my own health and my family's. I read everything I can, and I never sit in front of a doctor unprepared, because the informed patient gets different care and I have watched it change the outcome. It is the one kind of knowing I refuse to delegate, because the body it concerns is mine to look after.

But notice the verb. It says knowledge is power, not that it might become power. And that small word hides the entire problem.

CROSS-EXAMINATION

Knowledge is not power. Knowledge is potential power, the fuel and not the engine, and it does precisely nothing until you act on it.

Look honestly at where your life is actually stuck. For most of us, most of the time, the problem is not that we do not know what to do. We know we should rest, and we know the hard thing we keep not saying. The knowing is not missing. What is missing is the step from the knowing to the doing, and that step is where power actually lives. Knowledge that never crosses it is not power at all. It is informed paralysis, and it can sit heavier than plain ignorance, because it comes with the added weight of having known better.

There is a trap built into the saying for exactly this reason. "I need to learn more before I start" is the most respectable way in the world to never start. One more book, one more month of research, and the preparation that felt like progress turns out to have been a very dignified hiding place. The library card becomes somewhere to wait out the arena.

And the line was minted in an age when knowledge was scarce and hard to reach, which is no longer the age we live in. Now we drown in it. We can know everything about a problem by lunchtime and feel less able to act on it than when we knew nothing, because more knowing has curdled into more anxiety. The scarce and powerful skill is no longer gathering knowledge. It is discerning the little that matters and acting on it while ignoring the ocean that does not.

Knowledge really is the raw material of power, and an informed person is harder to push around, so the line is not wrong. It just stops one step too soon, at knowing, when the power was always waiting at doing.

A fuller, messier truth

Knowledge is not power. It is potential power, and the only thing that converts it is what you do next. The most informed person in the room is not the most powerful one. The most powerful one is whoever does something with what they know while everyone else is still researching. And here is the part worth sitting with: you probably already know enough. Not about everything, but about the thing you have been studying instead of starting. So learn, and learn hungrily, but keep one eye on the moment learning quietly stops being preparation and becomes the place you go to avoid beginning.

FEEL. PAUSE. ACT.

FEEL. Notice the hope the line gives you, the real dignity of knowing that learning is a door anyone can walk through. But notice too if there is a heaviness under it, the quiet weight of all the things you know you should do and have not. That weight is not laziness. It is unconverted knowledge, and it is telling you something.

PAUSE. Ask the question the saying lets you skip. Do I honestly need more information here, or do I already know enough to act, and "I need to learn more" has become the polite shape of my avoidance? Where am I using the library to hide from the arena?

ACT. Pick one thing you have been researching, or planning to understand better, rather than doing. Notice that you already know the first real step. Make the appointment. Send the email. Take that step this week, before you feel ready, because ready is mostly just the name we give the moment we run out of excuses to keep preparing. You are practicing converting one piece of known and unused knowledge into a single act, and closing, just once, the gap where all your power has been sitting.

§

Whether you already know enough to move on your particular thing depends on the thing, because sometimes you genuinely do need to learn more first. But you can feel the difference between honest preparation and elegant avoidance. The power was never in the knowing. It was always in the next thing you actually do.

THE EIGHTEENTH WITNESS

"You miss 100% of the shots you don't take."

DIRECT EXAMINATION

This one is a hand on your back, pushing you toward the thing you are afraid of. It names the hidden cost of playing it safe, the cost we almost never reckon, which is the guaranteed zero. The chance not pursued returns nothing, every time, with perfect reliability. For anyone frozen at the edge of an ask or a leap, this line cuts straight through the paralysis. The safe choice, the not-trying, is not actually safe. It is a loss you have agreed to in advance.

And there is truth in it. When people look back on their lives, the regrets that ache the longest are often the chances they never took, the rooms they never entered. Fear systematically lies to us, swelling the cost of trying and shrinking the cost of not, and this line is a loud, useful correction to a bias that quietly runs a lot of small lives.

But notice what the sentence measures, and what it conveniently leaves out. It tallies every shot you did not take. It says nothing whatsocver about the shots you take and miss, or about what those misses cost.

The line is a half-ledger, one column only.

Yes, you miss 100% of the shots you do not take. You also miss a sizable fraction of the shots you do take, and some of those misses are not free. They cost time you cannot get back, or an opportunity you spent on the wrong target and cannot spend again. The saying has the confident ring of a locker room because it tends to be repeated by the people who took the shot and scored. It does not poll the ones who took a similar shot and lost the house, because they are not the ones being quoted.

So taking every shot is not courage. It is noise, and sometimes it is ruin. The skill the line skips entirely is the one that actually matters, which is shot selection. The question was never simply take it or do not. It is whether this particular shot is worth what it costs, and whether you have sized the bet to something you could survive losing. Good risk-takers are not the people who shoot the most. They are the people who shoot well, and who can tell a real opportunity from a flattering distraction.

And here is the part the slogan cannot admit. Sometimes not taking the shot is the wise move. Some shots are bad bets that would cost far more than the prize is worth, and some you would only take to prove something to someone who is not even watching. The line treats every held shot as cowardice, when a good deal of it is judgment.

The shot you do not take is a guaranteed miss, and fear loves to dress that certain loss up as safety, so the line is telling a real truth. It is only half of one. The goal was never to take more shots. It was to take the right ones.

A fuller, messier truth

You do miss 100% of the shots you do not take, so when you are holding back out of fear, take the shot, because the not-taking is a certain loss wearing the mask of caution, and most of what people regret at the end is exactly this. But the line is only half the math. You also miss plenty of the shots you do take, and some of those misses cost more than the prize was ever worth. Courage was never taking every shot. It was taking the right ones, with your eyes open, sized to what you can afford to lose. Not every shot you are declining is cowardice. Some of it is judgment, and learning to tell those two apart is the whole game. Fear usually tries to keep you from exposure. Judgment tries to keep you from a cost that is not worth paying.

FEEL. PAUSE. ACT.

FEEL. When you find yourself not taking a shot, feel for what is actually stopping you. There is the hot, urgent flinch of fear, the one that wants you small and safe and will dress that up as being sensible. And there is the cooler, steadier read of judgment, the one that has quietly done the math and does not like the bet. They feel different in the body, and knowing which one is talking is where the answer starts.

PAUSE. Ask the questions the slogan skips. Am I not taking this shot out of fear, or out of genuine judgment? If I take it and miss, what does the miss actually cost me, and can I carry that? Is this a shot worth taking, or just a shot?

ACT. Take a shot you have been holding, and run it through two questions. First, am I avoiding this out of fear? If yes, the slogan is right, so name the fear plainly, because the not-taking is a loss you have already agreed to. Second, if I take it and miss, can I afford the cost? If the miss would be survivable, take it.

If the miss would be ruinous, then this is not a shot to take just because a slogan dared you to. Size it down to something you can survive, or pass on it with a clear conscience and no shame. If the shot is too costly as it stands, make it smaller. Send one inquiry before quitting the job. Test the idea before spending the savings. Have the conversation before making the irreversible move. You are practicing the thing the line forgot, telling the shots worth taking from the ones that only flatter you for being unafraid.

§

Whether to take your particular shot, I'll leave to you, because only you can weigh whether you are flinching or choosing, and only you know what a miss would cost you. But you can tell fear from judgment if you slow down enough to feel which is speaking. The goal was never more shots. It was the right ones.

THE NINETEENTH WITNESS

“The best way to predict the future is to create it.”

● DIRECT EXAMINATION

This one puts the pen in your hand. Instead of standing at the window anxiously forecasting what might be coming, you turn around and start building the thing you want to arrive. It is the great refusal of helplessness. The future is not weather that happens to you, it is a structure you put up, board by board, and the worry you would have spent guessing at it goes instead into making it. For anyone who has felt at the mercy of events, waiting to be chosen, waiting to see what fate decides, this line is a key turning in a lock. Stop predicting. Start building.

And it is some of the truest practical advice there is. A life usually changes more through action than through anxious forecasting. Worry is prediction with no hands. This line takes the same energy and gives it something to build with, and that shift alone has changed the direction of a great many lives.

But notice the verb it reaches for. Not influence the future, not tilt it. Create it, as though the whole thing were yours to author, as though no other hand were writing on the same page.

Here is the quiet overclaim. You do not create your future. You influence it, enormously, but you do not author it, because the future is co-written, and you are one writer in a crowded room.

You control your inputs. You do not control your outputs. You can do everything right, every board nailed true, and watch the outcome go the other way because of a market you did not move, or a body that had its own plans. And you can do very little and stumble into fortune you never built. The gap between effort and result is real, and it is permanent, and "create it" paves right over it as if it were not there.

That paving has a cost, and it comes due on the worst day. Because if you create your future, then the future you did not want is also your creation, your failure, your insufficient building. When the illness arrives, or the loss that no amount of foresight could have stopped, the gospel that felt so empowering turns and presents you with a bill. You take responsibility for a verdict you did not write alone, and you call your bad luck a personal defeat. The same belief, pointed outward, lets the fortunate decide they authored their own luck, and quietly tell the unlucky that they simply failed to create theirs.

The truth the line gets right is that proactivity beats passivity, every time, and that is not a small thing to get right. The error is only in the size of the word. Create implies authorship. Influence admits relationship, enormous but shared.

Building your future beats forecasting it, and the person with the hammer shapes more than the person at the window. None of that is the error. It is only that create promises authorship, when you author your efforts and never your outcomes, and a saying that forgets the difference hands you the blame for everything the world wrote on your page while you were not looking.

A fuller, messier truth

You cannot predict the future, and you cannot fully create it either, but you can influence it enormously, and all of that influence runs through what you actually do. So the instruction underneath is sound. Stop forecasting and start acting, because action shapes outcomes in a way worry never will.

But you author your efforts, not your results. The future is co-written, by you and by everything else that never read your plan, and a day comes for everyone when something lands that no amount of building could have stopped. If you believed you authored it all, that day breaks you, because you take the blame for a verdict written by other hands. So create the part that is yours, your actions, with everything you have. And hold the part that is not, the outcome, with an open hand.

FEEL. PAUSE. ACT.

FEEL. Notice the surge of ownership the line gives you, because that is the real antidote to helplessness and it is worth keeping. But notice too if there is a grip underneath it, the white-knuckled effort of someone who believes that if they only plan hard enough and control tightly enough, they can guarantee the result. That grip is exhausting, and it is information. It usually means you have started trying to author outcomes, not just inputs.

PAUSE. Ask the question the saying blurs. Am I confusing what I can do with what I can guarantee? Where am I taking responsibility for an outcome the world co-wrote? What is genuinely mine to create here, and what have I been straining to control that was never mine at all?

ACT. Take something you want in your future and split it down the middle. Draw two columns: Mine to do and Not mine to decide. Say the goal is a job you are reaching for. On one side go the inputs that are fully yours: the application you actually send, the people you reach out to, the way you prepare for the room. On the other side goes the one thing you cannot command, whether they choose you. In a relationship, your column may include honesty, repair, and how clearly you ask. The other column includes whether the other person receives it, changes, or stays.

Commit to the inputs completely, and schedule the first one this week. Then take the outcome and practice setting it down, out loud if it helps. "I will do all of this, and I cannot guarantee how it lands, and I am doing it anyway." You are practicing the move the saying skips, pouring yourself entirely into the part that is yours while loosening your grip on the part that never was.

§

What your future holds, I can't tell you, because no one creates it alone and none of us can see the other hands writing on the page. But you can tell the part that is yours to make from the part that is not, and the freedom is in giving everything to the first while you finally stop trying to control the second.

THE TWENTIETH WITNESS

"As I speak, so I create."

DIRECT EXAMINATION

This one names a power you have felt, even if you never put it this way. Words are not only description. They do things. Say "I am leaving" out loud and it becomes real in a way that thinking it for months never managed. Make a vow in front of a witness and you have rearranged your own future by speaking. The running commentary you keep up inside your head becomes, over years, the weather you live in. And there are words that change reality the instant they are spoken, I do, or I quit, not because of magic but because saying them is the act itself.

So the line is pointing at something true and old. Long before manifestation became an industry, cultures and scriptures understood that speech is a kind of making, and that naming a thing has force. Your voice is one of the few creative instruments handed out at birth, and "as I speak, so I create" honors that. The hope it stirs, that you could speak a better life into being, is reaching toward something real.

But notice how far the claim can be stretched, and how far the people selling it will stretch it. From your words shape your world, which is true, to your words bend the world directly, which is not.

Here is the line where a real truth becomes a profitable lie.

Words do not move matter by themselves. Saying “I am wealthy” deposits nothing. Speaking health over a tumor does not shrink it. Declaring abundance to the universe does not cover the rent, and the corner of the industry built on telling you otherwise is also, very quietly, telling the sick that they failed to speak themselves well and the broke that they manifested their own scarcity. That is the cruelty folded inside the magic. It takes “as I speak, so I create” to its logical end, and at that end stands a person who lost the thing they wanted being informed that they simply did not believe hard enough. It is victim-blaming with a vision board.

And it works the trick by cutting out the middle. Words really do create, but through a chain the magic conveniently deletes. What you say shapes your attention and your sense of who you are, which shapes what you actually do, which then, partly, shapes what happens. Word, to self, to action, to outcome. The manifestation version snips out the action in the middle and promises the outcome straight from the incantation, which is the oldest con there is, the harvest sold without the planting.

But do not overcorrect into believing your words are weightless, because that is its own error, and a colder one. Your words create constantly, just not by magic. They become the voice in your own head, the one still talking to you at three in the morning decades from now. Aimed at a child, they become the voice in theirs, for life. Sticks and stones was always a lie. You are building real interior worlds with your mouth every day, yours and other people’s, and that creation is not metaphorical at all.

You really do create with your words, genuinely and constantly. That part is true. It curdles into a lie, and in the wrong hands a racket, only when it forgets that words create through you and what you do, never over the world on their own.

None of this is aimed at prayer, or blessing, or a vow said out loud. Those can steady a person and give shape to what they mean to do. The con is only the version that promises the words will do it for you, with nothing asked of your own two hands.

A fuller, messier truth

You do create with your words, far more than you know, but not the way the saying is so often sold. Words do not bend the physical world, and anyone telling you they do is also telling the people who did not get what they wanted that they failed to say it hard enough.

But your words are creative in a deeper and realer way. They build the voice in your own head, and the voice in the heads of the people you speak to. They commit you, once a thing is said out loud and cannot be taken back. They set the frame you then act inside. Words create reality through you, by shaping who you become and what you do next, not on their own and not by magic.

So speak carefully, and speak boldly, because you are making something real with your mouth every day. Just never let the speaking stand in for the doing.

FEEL. PAUSE. ACT.

FEEL. Notice the hope the line stirs, the sense that your own voice could build you a life, because that hope is pointed at something true. But feel also for the magical version of it underneath, the wish that if you only say the right words enough times, the thing will arrive and spare you the work. That wish is the exact hook the whole manifestation machine is baited with, and it is worth catching in yourself, because it will quietly offer to let affirmation replace action.

PAUSE. Ask the question the saying hides. Am I speaking in order to commit myself and shape what I will actually do, or am I speaking instead of doing, hoping the words will do the doing for me? And the words I say the most, to myself and to the people I love, what are they actually building?

ACT. Two moves, because the power runs in two directions. First, the real creation: change one sentence you repeat often. Listen for the sentence you say to yourself most often, or the tone you most often use with one person you love, and shift one of those on purpose this week, because that reality genuinely is yours to make with words.

Second, the anti-magic: attach one spoken intention to one visible act. Take one thing you have been affirming or visualizing but not acting on, and bolt the words to a deed. Say the goal out loud, and then take the first real step the same day, so the speaking commits you to the work instead of excusing you from it.

§

Whether your words will get you what you want, I won't promise, because words alone never do that. But they shape who you become and what you do, which is the truest creative power you actually hold. So speak like it matters, because it does. And then go and do the thing the words just put your name to.

Where Am I Confusing Motion with Wisdom?

This count pushed you to act, and then asked you to aim. Before the final count, look at where your effort has been going.

What are you refusing to quit, and is it still worth what it takes from you?

Where are you mistaking motion for progress, or knowing for doing?

What outcome have you been holding yourself responsible for, that was never entirely yours to control?

You author your efforts, not your outcomes.

THE RULING

The ruling is ***yours.***

JURY ROOM

Use the space below to respond to the deliberation questions, record what surfaced, or put your ruling into words.

IN THE COURT OF CLARITY

COUNT SIX

THE PEOPLE,) CASE NO. 606692

Plaintiff,) JUDGE: YOU

v.

THE LARGE CLAIMS ABOUT TRUTH, FREEDOM, AND BEING RIGHT,

Defendant.

The charge: that they tempted you to stop looking the moment you felt sure.

Truth, Freedom, and Judgment

WITNESSES IN THIS COUNT

We are near the end now, and this count holds the largest claims in the book. Not rules for surviving a hard room or holding a relationship, but claims about how reality itself works: what truth does to you, how much of your life is yours to shape, whether circumstance is real or only a point of view, and what it means to be right. By now you have stood as judge again and again. This count is about judgment itself, and about its most seductive failure.

These sayings reach high, and each reaches for something real. Truth can free you. Happiness is partly yours to shape. A shift in perspective can change a life. Being right for its own sake really is a thin kind of wealth. At this altitude the sayings carry weight, which is exactly what makes them dangerous when they are incomplete, because a claim this large can wound precisely the people it fails to account for.

The truth will set you free leaves out that the truth usually costs you first. Freedom is on the far side of a fire, and the saying skips the fire. Happiness depends on ourselves quietly drops the word partly, and once that word is gone it starts blaming people for pain with causes far outside them. We are not victims of circumstance, we are victims of perspective treats every hard situation as a matter of mindset, which can talk a person out of a danger they should be walking away from. And being right is a poor man's version of wealth is the one that tempts you to close the whole inquiry the moment you feel right.

That last saying is why this count ends the book. Everything you have practiced has been a way of staying in the question a little longer, of not letting the comfortable verdict arrive too soon. This final saying whispers that you can stop now, that feeling right is the same as being done. It is not. Feeling right can be the most expensive place to stand when it costs you the humility to keep looking.

So this count keeps the gavel where it has belonged all along.

The question to carry through it is the one the whole book has been building toward:

THE QUESTION BEFORE YOU

When a belief leaves you feeling right, has it brought you closer to what is true, or only let you stop looking?

THE TWENTY-FIRST WITNESS

"The truth will set you free."

DIRECT EXAMINATION

The line began as scripture, in the Gospel of John, where Jesus is speaking about discipleship and a freedom far larger than honest disclosure. What most of us inherited is the looser, everyday version, the one about facing what is real and the relief that follows.

This one speaks straight to anyone who is tired of pretending. If you have ever carried a secret, or lived inside a story you knew was not quite true, you know the particular exhaustion of it, the low, constant labor of keeping the lie alive. "The truth will set you free" promises an exit from that. Put the performance down. Stop spending your energy guarding a version of events that was never going to hold. There is an open door, and on the other side of it you can finally breathe.

And the deep promise is true. Living a lie is its own slow prison, and denial often costs more over a life than honesty does. There is a real and profound freedom waiting on the far side of facing what is real, and people who finally tell the truth, or finally let themselves know it, often describe the relief in almost physical terms, like setting down something they had carried so long they forgot it had weight.

But notice what the sentence promises and what it quietly leaves out. It promises the freedom. It says nothing at all about the price of admission.

CROSS-EXAMINATION

Here is the part the line edits out. The truth will set you free eventually, but first it almost always wrecks something.

Tell the truth, the real one, and watch what happens before any freedom arrives. The comfortable arrangement comes apart. The image of yourself you had been carefully maintaining cracks down the middle. Face the truth you have been refusing, that the marriage is over, that the person you trusted hurt you, and the first thing it takes is not your chains. It is the protective story you were living inside. The freedom is real, but it sits on the far side of a fire, and the sentence shows you the far side while neatly cropping out the fire.

So people walk toward the truth expecting to feel lighter, and instead they feel the floor give way, and they conclude they have done something wrong. The truth was supposed to set me free, and instead it ruined everything. And too often they scramble back into the lie, not because the lie was better, but because nobody warned them that liberation has an invoice.

It helps to be honest about what the freedom even is. The truth does not free you from pain, and it does not free you from consequences. What it frees you from is the second job, the exhausting, around-the-clock labor of maintaining a version of reality that is not true. That is the real prize, and it is enormous, but it is not the painless gift the sentence implies. It is a trade. The sharp, immediate cost of the truth in exchange for the slow, grinding cost of the lie, paid out otherwise for the rest of your life.

The truth does free you, and the lie really is a prison. The promise underneath is sound. What the sentence hides is the cost: it sells you the destination and crops out the fire, and people who are not warned tend to turn back at exactly the wrong moment.

A fuller, messier truth

The truth will set you free, eventually, and living a lie is its own slow prison, so the promise underneath is real. But the truth almost always costs you something first. It takes the comfortable story before it gives you the open air, and what waits on the other side is not freedom from pain or consequence. It is freedom from the exhausting work of pretending. So tell the truth, face the truth, but walk in with your eyes open. You are not being handed a gift. You are making a trade, the cost of the truth now against the cost of the lie forever, and it is usually, though not always, the better deal.

FEEL. PAUSE. ACT.

FEEL. Notice the longing the line stirs, the wish to set the lie down and stop performing. That longing is honest, and it is worth listening to. But notice too if part of you flinches, already knowing what the truth will cost. That flinch is not cowardice. It is an accurate estimate of the bill, and you should let it speak before you decide anything.

PAUSE. Ask the questions the sentence skips. Am I expecting the truth to feel like freedom right away, when it may first feel like loss? Am I willing to pay what this particular truth costs on the way to whatever freedom is on the other side? And is this a truth I need to tell someone, or one I have been refusing to face in myself?

ACT. Take one truth you have been avoiding, and before you decide whether to move toward it, put two bills side by side on paper. First: what will the truth cost me now? Name it plainly, so the cost cannot ambush you later and send you fleeing back into the lie.

Second: what is the lie already costing me? The slow grind you have stopped noticing because you have paid it so long. Look at both. If the trade is worth it, take the first true step, say the sentence, or make the appointment, knowing you are walking toward freedom through the fire and not around it.

§

Whether to tell or face your particular truth is yours alone to weigh, because only you know what it will cost and whether you can carry it right now. But you can stop waiting for it to arrive as a clean gift, and you can decide, with open eyes, whether what stands on the far side of the fire is worth the walk.

THE TWENTY-SECOND WITNESS

"Happiness depends on ourselves."

DIRECT EXAMINATION

This one hands you back the keys. It says your wellbeing is not at the mercy of your circumstances or other people, that you are not stuck waiting for the right job or the right amount of money to finally arrive and make you happy. The source is inside you, and the inside is yours to tend. For anyone who has spent years outsourcing their happiness, pinning it on the next achievement and feeling the satisfaction evaporate a week after they got it, this line is a genuine liberation. Stop waiting on the world. Reclaim the thing.

And there is real truth here, the kind worth taking seriously. Put two people in similar circumstances and you may find two very different inner lives, because one of them has cultivated something the other has not. You do have real agency over where you place your attention, and over the meaning you build from what happens to you. That inner capacity is genuine, it can be strengthened, and people who have built it often have more room inside themselves when hardship comes than people who left their happiness entirely in the hands of conditions they could not control.

But notice the size of the claim. Not that happiness depends partly on us. That it depends on us, as though the rest of it, the whole world out there, did not get a vote.

CROSS-EXAMINATION

Here is where this gentle, empowering line can turn into one of the cruelest sentences a struggling person ever hears.

If happiness depends on you, fully, then anyone who is unhappy is failing at it. The logic is unavoidable, and it is brutal. Say it to a person ground down by poverty, by a depression that no reframe can lift, and you have just informed them that their suffering is a personal shortcoming, an attitude they are too weak or too foolish to correct. The same sentence that frees the comfortable can flog the afflicted. And it is convenient in an ugly way, because it lets everyone who is doing fine believe the miserable simply have bad attitudes, and it lets hard circumstances entirely off the hook.

It is worth being plain about one piece of this. Some unhappiness is not a mindset at all. Depression is an illness, not a failure of gratitude, and telling a sick person that their happiness depends on themselves can shame them out of the help that would actually reach it. There are kinds of suffering that no reframe touches, that need a doctor, or a change of conditions, rather than a better attitude.

So the line confuses a real thing with a false one. The real thing is that you have genuine agency over an inner portion of your life, and that portion is precious and worth tending fiercely. The false thing is that the inner portion is the whole thing. Happiness also depends, enormously, on whether you are safe and well, and whether you are loved, none of which you can fully attitude your way into.

Part of your happiness genuinely is yours to make, and reclaiming it is real freedom. The trouble is the one word the line drops, the word that keeps it honest, and in the wrong mouth that omission turns cruel: partly. Happiness depends partly on ourselves.

A fuller, messier truth

Happiness depends partly on you. There is an inner portion, your attention and the meaning you make, that is genuinely yours, and tending it is real work that real freedom comes from. But happiness also depends, hugely, on things you do not control, on whether your body is well and your life is safe. No attitude fully overrides a life in genuine crisis or a brain in genuine pain, and pretending it does is exactly how this kind-sounding sentence becomes a weapon against the people it is aimed at. So tend your portion fiercely, because it is real and it is yours. And refuse, absolutely, to be blamed for the part that was never yours to fix with mindset alone.

FEEL. PAUSE. ACT.

FEEL. Notice the empowerment the line offers, because reclaiming the part of your happiness that is genuinely yours is a real and freeing thing. But if instead it lands as a weight, if some part of you hears it as "so my unhappiness is my own fault," do not argue that feeling away. It may be telling you that you have been carrying responsibility for something that was never yours, or that something real, and not just your outlook, has been asking for your attention.

PAUSE. Ask the question the sentence flattens. Which part of my happiness is genuinely mine to tend, and which part is being set by conditions I do not control? And am I trying to fix with a better attitude something that actually needs to be changed, healed, or helped?

ACT. If you are carrying some unhappiness right now, sort it honestly into two piles. In one, the part you can genuinely tend, an attention you can redirect, a small habit within your reach. In the other, the part that is circumstance or biology, the part no reframe will fix. Mine to tend: the habit of rehearsing every slight before bed. Not mine to fix by mindset alone: a body in pain, a dangerous home, or a depression that needs care. Then give each the right remedy. Tend your portion with one real inner practice.

And for the other pile, stop trying to think your way out of it, and take one step toward what it actually needs, a doctor, the support of other people, or a change you have been avoiding. You are practicing the thing the saying refuses to do, telling the part that is yours from the part that is not.

§

How much of your happiness is yours to make, and how much the life around you sets, falls in a different place for every person, and I cannot see yours from here. But you can find it. Tend your part of it without apology. And refuse the blame for the part that was never yours alone.

THE TWENTY-THIRD WITNESS

"We are not victims of circumstance. We are victims of perspective."

DIRECT EXAMINATION

This one offers the most powerful freedom there is, the freedom that no situation can take from you. It says you are never truly trapped, because whatever has happened, the power to change your experience of it is always still in your hands, sitting in how you choose to see. For anyone who has felt pinned by their circumstances, this is a door that was apparently open the whole time. It seems to say no one can make you suffer without your participation. The last free country is the inside of your own head, and you hold its only passport.

And there is deep truth in it, the kind people have died affirming. The Stoics built a philosophy on the gap between what happens and what we make of it. Viktor Frankl found, inside a concentration camp, that the one thing his captors could not take was his freedom to choose his response. He did not mean that circumstance was irrelevant; he meant that even inside horrific circumstance, some last inner freedom remained. And in ordinary life it is simply, observably true that we often suffer far more than the facts require, dragging a single hard event through weeks of rehearsal, telling ourselves a story crueler than anything that actually happened. Reframing that kind of suffering is real, and it can change a life.

But notice how total the claim is. Not that we are sometimes victims of perspective. That we are not victims of circumstance at all, as though circumstance were never the culprit, as though nothing real were ever actually done to anyone.

CROSS-EXAMINATION

Here is where the most liberating sentence in the room can quietly become the most gaslighting one.

If you are never a victim of circumstance, only of perspective, then every pain you feel is a framing error, a thing you are doing to yourself. Say that to a person who was genuinely harmed, who was betrayed, or robbed of something that mattered, and you have performed a quiet act of cruelty. You have taken the fault out of the circumstance, where it belonged, and relocated it inside their own head. Your problem is not what was done to you. Your problem is your attitude about it.

That is not wisdom. It is the oldest move there is for silencing someone with a legitimate grievance, and it is beloved by exactly the people and institutions who would prefer your accurate perception of a real wrong to become, instead, your personal failure of outlook.

And there is a subtler danger, one that harms even when no one is weaponizing it. Sometimes the clear-eyed view that something is genuinely wrong is the precise thing trying to get you to change it. The dread about the job, the sense that a situation is quietly costing you your life, those are not always distortions to be reframed. Sometimes they are accurate readings, and your discomfort is the engine meant to move you. Reframe them away and you can talk yourself into staying calm inside a circumstance you were supposed to leave, now blaming yourself for ever having minded.

So the line collapses a real and necessary distinction. We do manufacture suffering on top of the facts, a great deal of it, and that manufactured layer genuinely is a perspective problem, and reframing it is freedom. But some suffering is not manufactured. It is the accurate, proportionate response to something that truly went wrong, and that suffering is not a flaw in your vision. It is your vision working correctly.

You are, often, a victim of perspective, and reclaiming that ground is real power. Where the line turns dangerous is its refusal to admit the rest: sometimes you are a genuine victim of circumstance, and a saying that denies that will eventually lie to you about which situation you are actually in.

A fuller, messier truth

You are sometimes a victim of perspective and sometimes a victim of circumstance, and the entire wisdom is in telling which. Perspective is real power. We pile suffering on top of the facts all the time, far more than the facts require, and reframing that added layer is some of the freest work a person can do.

But not all suffering is a framing error. Some of it is the accurate registration of a real wrong, and calling that a perspective problem does not free you, it gaslights you, and it can keep you sitting inside a harm you were meant to walk out of. So reframe the suffering you added. Honor the suffering that is telling the truth. And never let anyone, yourself included, use "it is just your perspective" to talk you out of seeing clearly.

FEEL. PAUSE. ACT.

FEEL. Notice the power the line offers, because the freedom to choose your response really is real, and on the right day it is everything. But if the line lands as a quiet accusation, if you hear it as "so this is my fault for how I am seeing it" about something that was genuinely done to you, do not reframe that feeling away. It may be the part of you that knows the harm was real and refuses to be talked out of it.

PAUSE. Ask the question the saying will not let you ask. How much of this pain is the accurate response to something genuinely wrong, and how much have I piled on top through the story I keep telling? And is "change your perspective" wisdom here, or is it sedating a clear view of something I actually need to act on?

ACT. Take a pain you are carrying and split it honestly. One part is the suffering the facts genuinely warrant, because something real is wrong, the grief a real loss earns, the anger a betrayal actually deserves. The other part is what you have added on top, the worst-case rerun you play at three in the morning, the version where it is all about you. The fact may be: this job is harming me. The added story may be: I am trapped forever.

For the added part, reframe it, and tell yourself a truer and fairer story on purpose. For the warranted part, do the opposite of reframing. Ask what it is trying to get you to do, and whether the honest answer is to change the circumstance rather than your view of it. You are practicing the move the saying skips, freeing yourself from the suffering you invented while refusing to explain away the suffering that is telling the truth.

§

Which of your pains is perspective and which is circumstance is not for me to sort, because only you know the difference between suffering you have inflated and suffering that is reporting a real wrong. But you get to keep both categories. Reframe what you added. And refuse, always, to let anyone reframe away what actually happened to you.

THE TWENTY-FOURTH WITNESS

"Being right is a poor man's version of wealth."

DIRECT EXAMINATION

This one arrives like a door opening onto fresh air, especially if you have spent years as the person who had to win. It names a trade you have almost certainly made and regretted, the argument won and the evening ruined, the point proved and the warmth gone out of the room. It says all that scorekeeping, all that energy spent being seen as correct, is a cheap and exhausting substitute for the things that actually make a life rich. Put down the need to be right, and you get back the peace and the strategic patience you were spending to feed your ego. The person who does not need to win every exchange is calmer, harder to manipulate, and very often the most powerful one in the room.

And there is real wisdom here, hard-won and Stoic in its bones. Most of what we fight to be right about does not matter, and the fighting costs us things that do. Win the argument, lose the marriage. Correct the tiny error in the meeting, lose the room. You know these trades, and you know they are bad ones. Letting the small rightness go is one of the quiet luxuries of a grown life.

But notice what the line does if you let it run all the way. It does not say being right about small things. It says being right, full stop, as though no rightness were ever worth its cost.

CROSS-EXAMINATION

Here is where this witness gets interesting, because it tempts you to stop doing the very thing you have been practicing all along.

Some things are worth being right about at absolutely any cost. Whether the diagnosis is correct. Whether a thing that someone insists did not happen actually happened. Being right about these is not ego. It is integrity, and sometimes it is survival, and a clever line that lumps it in with winning a dinner-table squabble is doing something worse than oversimplifying.

A world that has learned to call every insistence on truth a mere ego problem is a world being quietly talked out of reality, usually by whoever benefits from your no longer being sure. The phrase that frees you from petty point-scoring can, in the wrong hands, be used to walk you off the truth itself, and the people most eager to tell you that being right does not matter are very often the ones who would prefer you stopped being right about them.

So the line collapses the one distinction this whole book has been built to help you make. There is the rightness that is ego, the last word, the reflex to fix every small error in the room. That kind genuinely is a poor man's wealth, and dropping it makes you richer. And there is the rightness that is truth, the fact that actually matters, the thing you cannot abandon without abandoning what is real. Those two feel similar from the inside, both urgent and insistent, but one is your ego talking and the other is your integrity, and telling them apart is not a minor skill. It is the entire skill.

The need to win is a cheap imitation of a rich life, and putting it down is real freedom. At its worst, though, the line is a trap, because some rightness was never ego at all, and a saying that cannot tell the difference will eventually talk you out of the truths you most needed to keep.

A fuller, messier truth

The need to be right, the ego kind, the correcting-everyone kind, really is a poor man's version of wealth, and setting it down is one of the great quiet luxuries of a grown life. So drop the need to win. But do not, on the strength of a clever sentence, drop the truth along with it.

Some things are worth being right about at any cost, and a world that has learned to call all insistence on truth a character flaw is being slowly talked out of what is real. The wealth was never in winning, and it was never in surrendering either. It was in knowing the difference between a point you are defending because your ego is sitting on it, and a truth you are defending because it is true.

FEEL. PAUSE. ACT.

FEEL. Notice the relief the line offers, the permission to put down the exhausting scoreboard you have been carrying, because that relief is real and that scoreboard is heavy. But notice, too, if it is being used to talk you out of something you know is true, if there is a quiet "but this one actually matters" underneath the urge to just let it go. That quiet voice is not your ego. It is the part of you that still knows the difference, and it is worth listening to.

PAUSE. Ask the question you have learned to ask, now turned on being right itself. Am I holding onto being right out of ego, the last word and the need to look correct, or am I standing on something that is genuinely true and genuinely matters? Do I just want to win this, or does this one need to be kept? And what changes if I am right here?

ACT. The next time you feel the hot insistence of being right, sort it before you spend a single word. Am I trying to win, or am I trying to keep reality intact? If it is ego, the last word, the small correction no one needed, let it go on purpose, and feel the actual wealth of not having to win it.

Concede the point you would normally fight, and notice you lose nothing real. But if it is a truth that matters, a fact, a harm, a wrong that someone is trying to rewrite, hold it, kindly and immovably, and do not let any clever line about wealth and ego talk you off of what is real.

§

Which part of your rightness is ego and which is truth, I do not need to tell you, because by now you have had the practice. You have spent twenty-four sayings learning to make exactly this kind of distinction, to feel the pull, to pause and cross-examine it, and to decide for yourself what holds. Drop what is cheap. Keep what is true. That, in the end, was the whole of it.

JURY DELIBERATION · COUNT SIX

What Is Mine to Judge?

You have reached the largest questions, and you have been the judge the whole way here. This is the last deliberation before you carry the verdict off the page.

What truth have you been avoiding because some part of you senses it will cost you before it frees you?

Where have you blamed yourself for a circumstance whose causes ran far outside you?

The last time you were certain you were right, did it bring you closer to the truth, or only let you stop looking?

Being right is not the same as staying honest. Keep the question open a little longer.

THE RULING

The ruling is ***yours.***

JURY ROOM

Use the space below to respond to the deliberation questions, record what surfaced, or put your ruling into words.

THE VERDICT

Closing Argument

We have heard from twenty-four witnesses now. Sayings you have known your whole life, sentences that arrived before you could question them and got built into the walls of how you live. We put each one on the stand. We asked where it came from and what it was quietly leaving out, and in chapter after chapter we found the same strange thing. Almost none of them were lying to you. They were just telling you half.

So here, at the end, you might feel a little exposed. If family is not simply everything, and the heart does not get the final vote, then what exactly are you supposed to hold onto? It can feel, for a moment, as though the trial carried your furniture out and left the room bare.

It didn't. Look again. The sayings are all still here. "Family is everything" still has its warmth, and "never give up" still has its fire. Nothing was taken from you. What changed is your relationship to them. You used to swallow these lines whole, once, a long time ago, and live by whatever they happened to mean. Now you can pick one up when it fits the day and set it down when it is being used as a leash, because now you can tell the difference. That is not less than you started with. It is enormously more. You traded a stack of borrowed certainties for the one thing that is actually yours, which is judgment.

And you did not get it by reading. You got it by practicing. Two dozen times now you have done the same three moves, whether you noticed or not. You let yourself feel the pull of the saying, the warmth or the flinch it stirred, instead of rushing past it. You paused, and you cross-examined the thing instead of obeying it. And then you decided, for yourself, what to actually do. Feel. Pause. Act. It was never a slogan to memorize. It is a set of moves, and they are in your hands now, not on this page.

I want to say something plainly about the feeling, because it has been underneath all of this from the first chapter. Every saying in this book reached you first as a sensation, often before you had put a single thought to it. The softening or the tightening, the quiet yes or the small no in the body. The world will tell you that feeling is the unreliable part of you, the noise to be reasoned past, and a great deal of inherited advice is built on exactly that suspicion. But you have watched, again and again, what happens when you treat the feeling not as the enemy and not as the boss, but as the first witness. It got you to the question before your reasoning did, almost every time. Your job was never to silence it, and never simply to obey it. It was to read it. The feeling was the way in the whole time.

Which means the thing you may have spent a life trying to fix was never the malfunction. Being human, feeling all of it, the love and the grief and everything between, was always the instrument, not the breakdown. You do not have to earn your way out of being a person. You get to be one, on purpose, with your eyes open.

So I am not going to leave you with a new sentence to live by. That would be the one thing this whole book stood against, handing you a fresh slogan to swallow whole on your way out the door. You have had enough of those, and you know what to do with them now.

I am going to do the other thing instead.

I am going to hand you the gavel.

The verdicts in these pages were never mine to give. I told you what I thought, where each saying held and where it broke. But I was only ever a witness too. You are the judge. You always were. You are the only one who knows your fears and the exact weight these sayings have carried in your particular life. So keep what is true for you and leave the rest, then walk back out into your days as the one person finally qualified to rule on your own inherited wisdom.

Court is adjourned. ***Go live the verdict.***

THE TAKEAWAY

Feel. Pause. Act.

You have done this twenty-four times now. Here it is in one place, for the next time a saying lands on you and you are not sure whether to believe it.

FEEL. Notice what the advice does to you. Whether it settles something or sets your teeth on edge, that reaction is the first piece of information you get. You do not have to obey it, and you do not have to apologize for it. You have to read it. The feeling is telling you where to look.

PAUSE. Put the saying on the stand and ask it the questions you would ask any witness.

Is it true?

Is it always true?

Who taught me this, and what did it cost them?

What is it quietly leaving out?

Does it still serve the person I am now, or only the person I was when I first believed it?

ACT. Examination that stays in your head changes nothing. Keep what holds up. Revise what does not. Then do one small, concrete thing differently because of what you found. That is the difference between a belief you have looked at and a life you have changed.

The verdict, as always, is yours.

THE RECORD OF VERDICTS

The Twenty-Four Sayings, Retried

A word before you read this record. These are the verdicts I reached, one witness at a time, and I stood behind every one of them earlier in this book. They are not replacement sayings. The last thing I want is for you to tear out twenty-four old sentences and swallow twenty-four of mine whole. Keep this record the way a court keeps one: so you can come back later, put your ruling beneath the one read aloud that day, and see where your own life is the better authority. The verdict, as always, is yours.

1 *"Family is everything."*

Here is the version that survives cross-examination, and it is deliberately not as tidy as the original: Family is one of the most powerful forces in a life, strong enough to hold you up and strong enough to do lasting harm, which is the exact reason it cannot be everything. Blood can explain the bond, though plenty of real families are chosen rather than born. History deepens it, and love can make it sacred. But none of those things removes the need for terms. Family does not stop being family because you name what you can and cannot carry. Sometimes terms are the only way love survives without turning into injury. That does not fit on a coffee mug, and that is the point. The original was clean because it was incomplete. The truth has edges.

My ruling:

2 *"Good people put others first."*

Good people care for others and count themselves among the people who deserve care. Generosity is not measured by how much of yourself disappears in the giving. It is measured by whether the giving is chosen, honest, and sustainable. The virtue lives in the narrow middle, where you give from enough instead of from empty, and where your own need is not treated as an embarrassing interruption in everyone else's life. The aim was never to put yourself first every time. It was to stop pretending you are not in the room.

My ruling:

3 *“When your past calls, don’t answer. It has nothing new to say.”*

The past isn’t always trying to drag you back. Sometimes it is just trying to be understood. So when it calls, find out which call it is. If it is only there to hurt you again, let it ring. But if it keeps returning in the same recurring fight and the same familiar ache, answer it once, long enough to learn what it came to say, and then come back to the present. The skill is the difference between a phone call and a forwarding address. You are allowed to listen. You are not required to move in.

My ruling:

4 *"Never let them see you sweat."*

There are places where you should never let them see you sweat, and whoever taught you this was right about them. The negotiation, the table where showing fear gets you eaten. But a person who treats every encounter as enemy territory spends an entire life in armor. The real skill was always knowing which is which. The part that may never have been taught to you is that some rooms are safe enough, and in those the brave thing, the genuinely strong thing, is to let someone see you sweat.

My ruling:

5 *"They should never see you coming."*

There are arenas where they should never see you coming, and the surprise really is your edge, and you were smart to use it. But surprise was always a tactic, not an address. A person no one ever sees coming is also a person no one ever truly sees. Stay invisible in the rooms you have to win that way. But somewhere, with someone, let yourself be seen arriving, on purpose, as exactly who you are. Being underestimated is a weapon. It was never meant to be a home.

My ruling:

6 *"Walk softly but carry a big stick."*

Walking softly with strength in reserve is real wisdom, and the point of carrying a big stick was always so that you would not have to swing it. But a stick you can never put down stops being a tool and becomes a tax you pay on every step, and a person who is always armed cannot be soft with anyone, including the people who would never make them fight. The strength was in having the stick. The freedom is in knowing it can lean against the wall while you sit down.

My ruling:

7 *"My education is my trust fund."*

Your education really is a trust fund, the one inheritance no one can take from you, and whoever taught you this was likely right about the world they were preparing you to survive. But a trust fund is something you live off, and an education is something you live in. Treat it only as security and you turn a door into a wall. It was meant to make you harder to dismiss, yes, and also more curious, and more able to say "I don't know" without feeling your worth drop a single point. The richest version of you is not the one who banked the most. It is the one who never stopped spending it on curiosity.

My ruling:

8 *"Failure is not an option."*

There are moments where failure is not an option, and your crossing may well have been one of them, and the person who told you so was telling you the truth about the world you had just landed in. But that rule was for the crossing, not for the whole of the life on the other side. Once you are safe, failure stops being the enemy and becomes the curriculum. The people who build the most are not the ones with no failures behind them. They are the ones who made failing survivable enough that they could afford to attempt the things that mattered. The aim was never a life with no failure in it. It was a life large enough to hold some.

My ruling:

9 *"Follow your heart."*

Your heart is one of the truest witnesses you have, and you should never put it on mute, because it knows things your reasoning will keep denying for years. But a witness is not a verdict. Let your heart testify in full, and then let the rest of you cross-examine it, your hard-won memory of where this certainty led the last time, and the people who love you and have no reason to lie. The heart was never built to drive the car alone. It was built to tell you, loudly and honestly, where you actually want to go. Then you, the whole of you, decide whether to go there.

My ruling:

10 *"Trust your gut."*

Trust your gut, and then ask it the one question it will never volunteer: where did you learn this? When the read is about danger, act first and audit later, because that is the one arena where the cost of being slow is too high. But when it is a snap judgment about a person or a path, make the certainty show its papers before you let it decide. A gut schooled on real experience is faster than your reasoning and worth following. A gut schooled on fear is only fear that learned to sound sure. The feeling is the same. The schooling is everything.

My ruling:

11 *"I think, therefore I am."*

You are not only because you think. You are also when you ache, when you are held, when you are so absorbed in a thing that you forget to narrate yourself at all. The mind is a magnificent instrument and a poor master, and some of the realest hours of your life were the ones where the thinking finally went quiet. A baby exists before its first sentence. You did too, and you still do, in every moment you are not explaining.

My ruling:

12 *"Everything happens for a reason."*

You cannot always find a reason in what happened. About the worst things, there may be no reason that any decent person would accept. But in time, you may be able to make meaning from it, and that is the part the saying gets backward. The meaning is not waiting inside the event like a prize you have to dig out. It is something you build afterward, with your own hands, out of the wreckage, and the fact that you built it is precisely what makes it real and yours. Not everything happens for a reason. But almost nothing has to stay meaningless, if you are the one who decides to make something of it. If your faith tells you a reason exists, that belief is yours to hold, and this chapter is not here to take it from you. The harm starts somewhere else: when another person assigns the reason to your loss, or when you force one onto yourself before your grief has had its hearing.

My ruling:

13 *"Look on the bright side."*

The bright side is a real place, and there are days when getting there is what saves you. But it is a destination, not a detour around the feeling, and it only holds your weight if you reached it by walking through the dark side rather than leaping over it. So look on the bright side, yes, but after you have looked, honestly and without hurrying, at the actual one. The order is the whole thing. Let what happened have its hearing first, and then, if you choose, turn toward the light, having already heard what the dark was trying to tell you. The bright side is not false. It is just not first.

My ruling:

14 *"What doesn't kill you makes you stronger."*

Some of what doesn't kill you makes you stronger. Some of it just leaves you tired, or quieter than you used to be, and surviving is not the same as being improved. Pain may reveal strength, but recovery is what builds it. When strength does rise out of a hard thing, it does not rise from the thing itself. It comes from what you did afterward, and who stood with you while you did it. So do not thank the wound. Thank the healing, thank the people who helped you heal, and give yourself the credit for the work. And never go hunting for a fire because you have been told it will forge you. Plenty of fires only burn.

My ruling:

15 *"Time heals all wounds."*

Time is the soil. It is not the gardener. Fresh pain dulls with time, so do not rush yourself, but a wound only heals if something tends it, and the tending is yours to do. And the deepest wounds do not vanish even when you tend them beautifully. You do not get over the great losses. You grow around them, slowly, until they sit inside a life grown wide enough to hold them. The wound will still ache on certain days, and that is not failure. That is the shape love takes once it has nowhere left to go.

My ruling:

16 *"Never give up."*

Persistence is a superpower, and most people really do quit a step before the turn, so when the goal is right, never give up is close to gospel. But never is a lie, because the wisest and bravest thing you ever do might be to stop. The skill the saying refuses to teach is the hard one, telling the difference between hard-because-it-is-worth-it and hard-because-it-is-wrong. Hard-and-right may tire you, but it still points toward a life you want. Hard-and-wrong drains you while asking you to call the draining devotion. Push through the first with everything you have. Walk away from the second without calling it failure. Quitting the wrong thing is not giving up. It is giving the right thing your life back.

My ruling:

17 *"Knowledge is power."*

Knowledge is not power. It is potential power, and the only thing that converts it is what you do next. The most informed person in the room is not the most powerful one. The most powerful one is whoever does something with what they know while everyone else is still researching. And here is the part worth sitting with: you probably already know enough. Not about everything, but about the thing you have been studying instead of starting. So learn, and learn hungrily, but keep one eye on the moment learning quietly stops being preparation and becomes the place you go to avoid beginning.

My ruling:

18 *"You miss 100% of the shots you don't take."*

You do miss 100% of the shots you do not take, so when you are holding back out of fear, take the shot, because the not-taking is a certain loss wearing the mask of caution, and most of what people regret at the end is exactly this. But the line is only half the math. You also miss plenty of the shots you do take, and some of those misses cost more than the prize was ever worth. Courage was never taking every shot. It was taking the right ones, with your eyes open, sized to what you can afford to lose. Not every shot you are declining is cowardice. Some of it is judgment, and learning to tell those two apart is the whole game. Fear usually tries to keep you from exposure. Judgment tries to keep you from a cost that is not worth paying.

My ruling:

19 *"The best way to predict the future is to create it."*

You cannot predict the future, and you cannot fully create it either, but you can influence it enormously, and all of that influence runs through what you actually do. So the instruction underneath is sound. Stop forecasting and start acting, because action shapes outcomes in a way worry never will. But you author your efforts, not your results. The future is co-written, by you and by everything else that never read your plan, and a day comes for everyone when something lands that no amount of building could have stopped. If you believed you authored it all, that day breaks you, because you take the blame for a verdict written by other hands. So create the part that is yours, your actions, with everything you have. And hold the part that is not, the outcome, with an open hand.

My ruling:

20 *"As I speak, so I create."*

You do create with your words, far more than you know, but not the way the saying is so often sold. Words do not bend the physical world, and anyone telling you they do is also telling the people who did not get what they wanted that they failed to say it hard enough. But your words are creative in a deeper and realer way. They build the voice in your own head, and the voice in the heads of the people you speak to. They commit you, once a thing is said out loud and cannot be taken back. They set the frame you then act inside. Words create reality through you, by shaping who you become and what you do next, not on their own and not by magic. So speak carefully, and speak boldly, because you are making something real with your mouth every day. Just never let the speaking stand in for the doing.

My ruling:

21 *"The truth will set you free."*

The truth will set you free, eventually, and living a lie is its own slow prison, so the promise underneath is real. But the truth almost always costs you something first. It takes the comfortable story before it gives you the open air, and what waits on the other side is not freedom from pain or consequence. It is freedom from the exhausting work of pretending. So tell the truth, face the truth, but walk in with your eyes open. You are not being handed a gift. You are making a trade, the cost of the truth now against the cost of the lie forever, and it is usually, though not always, the better deal.

My ruling:

22 *"Happiness depends on ourselves."*

Happiness depends partly on you. There is an inner portion, your attention and the meaning you make, that is genuinely yours, and tending it is real work that real freedom comes from. But happiness also depends, hugely, on things you do not control, on whether your body is well and your life is safe. No attitude fully overrides a life in genuine crisis or a brain in genuine pain, and pretending it does is exactly how this kind-sounding sentence becomes a weapon against the people it is aimed at. So tend your portion fiercely, because it is real and it is yours. And refuse, absolutely, to be blamed for the part that was never yours to fix with mindset alone.

My ruling:

23 *"We are not victims of circumstance, we are victims of perspective."*

You are sometimes a victim of perspective and sometimes a victim of circumstance, and the entire wisdom is in telling which. Perspective is real power. We pile suffering on top of the facts all the time, far more than the facts require, and reframing that added layer is some of the freest work a person can do. But not all suffering is a framing error. Some of it is the accurate registration of a real wrong, and calling that a perspective problem does not free you, it gaslights you, and it can keep you sitting inside a harm you were meant to walk out of. So reframe the suffering you added. Honor the suffering that is telling the truth. And never let anyone, yourself included, use "it is just your perspective" to talk you out of seeing clearly.

My ruling:

24 *"Being right is a poor man's version of wealth."*

The need to be right, the ego kind, the correcting-everyone kind, really is a poor man's version of wealth, and setting it down is one of the great quiet luxuries of a grown life. So drop the need to win. But do not, on the strength of a clever sentence, drop the truth along with it. Some things are worth being right about at any cost, and a world that has learned to call all insistence on truth a character flaw is being slowly talked out of what is real. The wealth was never in winning, and it was never in surrendering either. It was in knowing the difference between a point you are defending because your ego is sitting on it, and a truth you are defending because it is true.

My ruling:

YOUR OWN DOCKET

Put One Belief on Trial

Twenty-four witnesses have taken the stand. Now the docket is yours.

Somewhere in you is a sentence this book never called: the one your family said at the table, the one a coach or a boss installed, the one you have repeated so long you forgot it was ever handed to you. Put one of them on trial here. The procedure is the one you have now practiced twenty-four times, and the open space that follows is deliberate. This is your courtroom.

IN THE COURT OF CLARITY

THE PEOPLE,	)
Plaintiff,	) CASE NO.
v.	) JUDGE: YOU
THE BELIEF YOU CARRY,	)
Defendant.	)

The charge: **to be determined by the court.**

The saying on trial:

“ ”

DIRECT EXAMINATION

Let the saying make its best case. It has one, or it would never have lasted this long.

Who handed you this sentence, and what world were they trying to survive when they learned it?

What has it protected you from, or gotten you through?

What do you feel in your body when you say it out loud? That is testimony. Write it down.

CROSS-EXAMINATION

Now put it under oath. Ask it the questions you would ask any witness.

Is it true?

Is it always true?

Who taught me this, and what did it cost them?

What is it quietly leaving out?

Does it still serve the person I am now, or only the person I was when I first believed it?

A fuller, messier truth

Write the version that survives your cross-examination. It will be longer than the original, and it will not fit on a coffee mug. That is how you know it is yours.

FEEL. PAUSE. ACT.

The feeling took the stand in your direct examination. The pause was the five questions. What remains is the act.

Because of what I found, this week I will

THE RULING

My ruling:

The ruling is yours. It always was.

CONVENE THE COURT

A Guide for Reading Groups

This book was built for one juror at a time, but sayings are social things. They were handed to us by other people, usually out loud, and there is something fitting about examining them the same way. Six sessions follow, one for each count, each anchored to the deliberation question your members will already have answered alone in the jury room. The group's job is not to reach one verdict. Twelve jurors, twelve rulings. The job is to let everyone hear how differently the same sentence can land in different lives, because nothing loosens a saying's grip faster than discovering the person next to you inherited the opposite one.

A word for the room before the first session. The saying is on trial, not the person speaking. Nobody cross-examines anybody else's life here, and nobody hands down a verdict on it either. When someone shares, listen for what the sentence protected and what it cost, and let that be enough. Anyone may pass. What is said in the jury room stays in the jury room. And when the room disagrees, good: that is the evidence arriving.

Two assignments before the first session: ask each member to bring the saying they heard most growing up, whether or not it appears in this book. You will need them in session six. Ask them to bring their jury room pages as well, not to read aloud but so the work each member did alone is in the room with them.

SESSION ONE

Love and Loyalty (Chapters 1-3)

Anchor: What did love teach me to carry?

Which of the three sayings in this count was said in your house, and in whose voice do you still hear it?

Joy writes that "but they're family" has closed more honest conversations than almost any phrase we own. What conversation did it close in your life, and what would reopening it cost?

Where did the group split: who heard these sayings as warmth, and who heard them as a leash?

Closing question: What did tonight's testimony change about who you owe, and how much?

SESSION TWO

Survival and Armor (Chapters 4-8)

Anchor: What armor am I still wearing?

Five pieces of armor testify in this count. Which one did you recognize as your own before you finished the sentence?

Did anyone else in the room pick the same armor for a completely different reason?

Who handed you your armor, and what were they surviving when they learned to wear it?

The count asks whether the war is over. How would someone who loves you answer that about you?

Closing question: What is one room where you may no longer need the armor you keep reaching for?

SESSION THREE

Heart, Gut, and Mind (Chapters 9–11)

Anchor: Which inner voice have I let rule?

Go around the room once. Heart, gut, or mind: which one usually gets your last word?

Tell the group about one time your crowned voice was wrong, and what the demoted voices had been trying to say.

Joy calls the feeling the first witness. What changes in a hard decision if you treat it as testimony instead of a verdict?

Closing question: Which inner voice gets a fuller hearing from you this week?

SESSION FOUR

Pain and Meaning (Chapters 12–15)

Anchor: What have I been asked to call healing?

Which of these four sayings has been said to you in fresh pain, and what did you need to hear instead?

The count draws a line between comforting someone and rushing them. Where has your group seen that line crossed?

What would it sound like to sit with someone in pain without handing them a saying at all? Try writing the first sentence together.

Closing question: What pain in your life needs less explanation and more tending?

SESSION FIVE

Ambition, Action, and Creation (Chapters 16-20)

Anchor: Where am I confusing motion with wisdom?

What are you refusing to quit, and what did the group hear in how you described it?

Joy's verdict is that you author your efforts, not your outcomes. Which outcome have you been grading yourself on, and what would the effort grade be instead?

Where has hustle language been used on you by someone who benefited from your motion?

Where have you used motion to avoid a harder kind of honesty?

Closing question: What is one action worth taking, and one motion worth stopping?

SESSION SIX

Truth, Freedom, and Judgment (Chapters 21-24), and closing

Anchor: What is mine to judge?

Bring out the sayings collected before session one. Put one on the stand together, live: its best case, its cross-examination, its fuller and messier truth. Let the room disagree, and notice that the disagreement is the point.

The book ends by handing you the gavel. Name one inherited sentence you are keeping on purpose, with your eyes open, and one you are setting down.

Then close the way the book closes. Court is adjourned. Go live the verdict.

WHEN THIS BOOK IS NOT ENOUGH

This book was written to help you examine inherited wisdom, not to replace the help some situations require.

If a chapter brought something to the surface, grief or fear or a truth you are not sure how to face, take that seriously. The reaction is information. It may also be a sign that the next step is not one to take alone.

If you are in immediate danger, or if you may harm yourself or someone else, contact emergency services or a current crisis line where you live.

If what surfaced feels connected to trauma, depression, grief, or a relationship that does not feel safe, a licensed professional can reach what a book cannot.

If what surfaced involves a medical, legal, or financial decision, do not let this book be your only counsel. Get advice from someone qualified in your particular situation.

And if you are reading with a group: the saying is on trial, not the person speaking. No one owes the room a disclosure, and no one should be cross-examined about their pain.

Feel. Pause. Act. is a practice of telling things apart.
Sometimes the clearest act is asking for help.

GRATITUDE

Acknowledgments

To my colleagues at the Law Offices of Stephenson, Acquisto & Colman and at Proactive Health Labs, thank you for the room to write something that lives outside the day's work.

ABOUT THE AUTHOR

Joy Stephenson-Laws

Joy Stephenson-Laws has spent more than forty years as a healthcare attorney, and the habit that work built in her runs through this book: the conviction that the claim everyone accepts without question is the one most worth examining. She is the founding and managing partner of the Law Offices of Stephenson, Acquisto & Colman, a healthcare litigation firm with a national practice.

She is also the founder and president of Proactive Health Labs, a nonprofit devoted to evidence-based health education, and a certified holistic life coach. Her work, in law and in health education alike, returns to a single idea: that people do better when they are handed the tools to question what they have been told and decide for themselves. She is the author of *Your Labs Are Fine. You're Not.*; *Secrets That Sparkle (and Secrets That Sting)*; *From Chains to Wings: A Poetry Revolution for Healing*; and *Minerals: The Forgotten Nutrient.*

Joy grew up on a farm in Jamaica before immigrating to California, and she carried with her the survival wisdom her mother handed down, much of which turns up in these pages. This book is, in part, her way of going back to examine what she was given, and of showing that you can question the advice that saved you without betraying the person who gave it to you.

To learn more, visit the Learning Lab at **phlabs.org/education.**

www.ingramcontent.com/pod-product-compliance
Lightning Source LLC
LaVergne TN
LVHW051055210926
848486LV00002B/116
* 9 7 9 8 9 9 3 9 7 4 0 8 8 *